THE GLASS SUPPER

by Martyn Hesford

Published by Playdead Press 2014

© Martyn Hesford 2014

Martyn Hesford has asserted his rights under the
Copyright, Design and Patents Act, 1988, to be identified
as the author of this work.

A CIP catalogue record for this book is available from the
British Library.

ISBN 978-1-910067-16-1

Printed by BPUK

Playdead Press
www.playdeadpress.com

The Glass Supper was first performed at the Hampstead Theatre on Wednesday 25th June 2014. The cast was as follows:

Cast:

Marcus	Michael Begley
Colin	Owen Sharpe
Wendy	Michelle Collins
Steven	Michael Feast
Jamie	Alex Lawther

Creative:

Writer	Martyn Hesford
Director	Abbey Wright
Designer	Signe Beckmann
Lighting	David Plater
Sound and Music	Harry Blake

The Glass Supper

The Glass Supper takes place in different worlds. The outside world that we see, and the inside world that we feel. Everything seems to be real on the surface. We present ourselves to the world as one thing, don't we? But inside we are a mass of contradictions. Different feelings, different people, all happening at the same time, in the one moment. We hide our fears, truths and secrets, but sometimes these truths bubble up, they appear on the surface. We can never run away from ourselves, can we? Not if we want to know who and what we are. We must face ourselves one day. Face the life we have created for ourselves. The play is like watching tropical fish in a fish tank. Through the glass of the aquarium, we see into the underwater world. We watch the fish swimming around and around. Going where? Doing what? Existing. The play also has another world, a world that comes through from time to time, to remind us that we're not that important. We can sometimes hear that world in the sound of a church bell, a sigh, the silence... It's the eternal.

Martyn Hesford

For Keith

CAST

Marcus (37)
Colin   (38)

Jamie   (18)

Steven (50)
Wendy (50)

London/Essex accents

ACT 1 SCENE ONE

*Light slowly appears. **COLIN** (38) sits. **MARCUS** (37) stands. Four figures stand in the background - shadows - **STEVEN** (50), **WENDY** (50), **JAMIE** (18)*

(SILENCE)

MARCUS   Look at me.

COLIN   No.

MARCUS   I said look at me.

(Colin closes his eyes)

COLIN   You notice the quiet, don't you, when we're together? The silence.

MARCUS   Yes.

COLIN   I like it here with you. Do you - with no-one else?

(Opens eyes)

Don't go away.

MARCUS   Look at me.

(PAUSE)

I said look at me.

(Colin looks at Marcus)

COLIN   I'm sorry.

7

(*PAUSE*)

> I've stopped. This is the last time. I've stopped. Honest. Promise. I promise. I've stopped.

(*He closes his eyes*)

(*Softly*)

> Do you think Jesus is in this house?

(*Music. A long, sharp, searing note. Glass-like/angel-like. Piercing*)

(*Light fades*)

SCENE TWO

(*Lights up*)

(*A living room. Marcus, Colin, Jamie, Steven and Wendy stand*)

STEVEN   How are you? How are you both? How are you?

COLIN   We're fine. Both fine. Aren't we?

MARCUS   Yes, we are. We're both fine.

JAMIE   Good.

STEVEN   Good. That's good.

COLIN   And you? How are you?

STEVEN   We're fine.

JAMIE   Yes, we're fine, too.

COLIN   That's good. Very good.

MARCUS   Good.

WENDY   Hello.

(*She waves*)

MARCUS   Hello?

COLIN   You found us then?

STEVEN   Yes, we found you, in a fashion.

WENDY	The Tom Tom.
JAMIE	Yeah, the Tom Tom. it took us near a church, didn't it? A cemetery.
WENDY	Spooky. I was dead nervy. I'm not used to cemeteries. Spooky. Dead spooky.

(*She waves*)

	Hiya.
MARCUS	Who's this?
WENDY	Me?
COLIN	Yes, who's this?
STEVEN	This is Wendy.
WENDY	I'm Wendy. Hiya.
COLIN	Hello.
MARCUS	Hello.
WENDY	Hiya. Nice to meet you. I've heard a lot about you both.
COLIN	Really?
WENDY	Oh yes.

(*She shakes hands with Colin and Marcus*)

STEVEN	We hope you don't mind.
COLIN	Mind?

STEVEN   Us turning up like this.

WENDY   With me.

MARCUS   You?

JAMIE   Wendy.

WENDY   Hiya.

(*She waves*)

STEVEN   She's coming with us, you see.

WENDY   Yes.

STEVEN   It was all very last minute.

WENDY   Oh yes, very last minute.

STEVEN   Yes.

JAMIE   She's very lucky.

WENDY   Oh yes, I'm very lucky. I'm ever so excited.
It's my first time, you see.

COLIN   Your first time?

WENDY   We're going on holiday.

JAMIE   A cruise.

STEVEN   The Queen Mary.

WENDY   The three of us.

JAMIE   Together.

WENDY	Isn't it exciting. I'm ever so excited. I can't wait.
STEVEN	Sail tomorrow, from Southampton.
WENDY	I've never been on a ship before in my life.
STEVEN	Ocean liner.
WENDY	I've only been on a ferry crossing. River Mersey, with my Auntie Mary.
STEVEN	You don't mind us turning up like this, do you? Uninvited. On speck, so to speak.

(*Colin and Marcus, saying nothing, look at each other*)

JAMIE	We said we should do it, meet up again, didn't we?
COLIN	Yes.
MARCUS	Yes, we did.
JAMIE	Well then, here we are.
WENDY	Surprise surprise.
STEVEN	Marvellous.
COLIN	Yes.
MARCUS	Yes.
WENDY	We're staying in a hotel tonight, in Southampton. The De Vere. All mod cons.

12

| STEVEN | Yes, just breaking up our journey for an hour or two. Just saying hello. |

WENDY

(*Waves*)

Hiya.

| COLIN | Great. |

(*PAUSE*)

| MARCUS | Let me take your coats. |
| WENDY | Ta. |

(*Wendy is glamorously dressed, but everything is Essex overdone - hair, make-up, false eyelashes, nails, shoes (like an over-dressed Christmas tree.) She takes off jacket, a fun fur. She reveals a very low cut, sparkling, over the top blouse - sexy. She waits for Marcus and Colin's reaction. They react*)

COLIN	Wow.
MARCUS	Oh.
WENDY	Nice, i'n it?
COLIN	Very.
WENDY	Bought it especially.

(*Marcus takes coats*)

Yes, seven nights. Six days. Over to New York. Atlantic crossing on the Queen Mary.

I've never been to New York. All those glass buildings, the shopping, I can't wait. I've googled everything in advance. It looks very upmarket, the Queen Mary. Very selective. Posh.

STEVEN Standards. High class clientele.

(*Marcus leaves with coats*)

WENDY I'm a bit nervous, actually. I hope I'll fit in.

STEVEN You'll be fine, won't she, Jamie?

JAMIE Yes, especially in that blouse. Most definitely.

WENDY I hope so. I don't want to stand out for all the wrong reasons, do I? These two are used to it, posh things, aren't you, boys, wearing black tie and that?

STEVEN You'll be fine, won't she?

JAMIE She will

WENDY Good. I'm sure they'll tell me if I put a foot wrong, won't you?

JAMIE We will.

(*PAUSE*)

COLIN (*Smiles*) Sit yourself down.

14

WENDY   Thanks.

(*They sit*)

STEVEN   So, this is it, where you live, Colin.

COLIN   Yes. We moved in six months ago.

(*Marcus enters*)

STEVEN   Nice house, Marcus.

MARCUS   Cottage, actually.

WENDY   Yes, it's beautiful, isn't it? Very me is this, a house in the country.

STEVEN   Cottage, Wendy.

(*Far away, wind chimes blow, outside*)

WENDY   Oh, what's that?

MARCUS   The wind chimes.

WENDY   Oh, how nice. That's nice. Wind chimes, Steven, they've got everything, haven't they?

STEVEN   Yes, very nice; it is.

JAMIE   An atmosphere.

STEVEN   Homely.

WENDY   Very.

COLIN   What's everybody drinking?

MARCUS	(*Slightly put out*) Oh? Are we drinking?
COLIN	Well, yes. We've got guests, haven't we? (*Smiles*) What you having?
STEVEN	(*Smiles*) What you got?
COLIN	Wine?
STEVEN	Lovely.
JAMIE	Great.
WENDY	Fabulous.
COLIN	Red or white?
WENDY	Both. We don't mind what we have, do we, Steven? We drink anything. We're not fussed.
MARCUS	(*Put out*) Good.

(*BLACKOUT*)

SCENE THREE

(*Colin, Steven, Jamie, Wendy, drink wine. Marcus stands drinking water*)

STEVEN   Very nice, is this.

WENDY   Oh, gorgeous, it is. (*Sips*) Oh, I could get used to this. Any time of the day. Fruity.

COLIN   (*Drinks*) Cheers.

STE./JAMIE   Cheers.

STEVEN   How we found you, I don't know. How do you manage, living out here, cut off from anyone?

JAMIE   We didn't see a soul for ages, mate.

WENDY   Ever so lonely, I bet.

MARCUS   Actually, we like it, don't we, Colin? Living in the middle of nowhere.

COLIN   Yes, we do.

MARCUS   It was the main reason for buying the place, you see. Getting out of London. Living on our own.

WENDY   Really?

STEVEN   Why was that?

MARCUS   Lots of reasons.

WENDY	I bet you've both got a nice car, though, haven't you? You'd need the right car living out here, wouldn't they, Steven?
STEVEN	Oh yes. Naturally.
MARCUS	Actually, I don't drive.
WENDY	You don't drive?
MARCUS	No, never learnt, did I, Colin?
COLIN	No.
JAMIE	Why not, Marcus?
COLIN	His nerves.
MARCUS	No it's not. It's my concentration. If I see anything diverting - rabbits, monkjacks, badgers - I'm off.
STEVEN	Really?
MARCUS	Yes. Daydreaming.
COLIN	It's his job, you see.
MARCUS	The writing. Imagination.
WENDY	Really?
(*PAUSE*)	
	Well, I'd be lost without a car. It's a necessity for shopping and things, isn't it, Steven?

18

MARCUS	We've no shops here. No pub either.
WENDY	No pub?
COLIN	Nothing.
MARCUS	Five miles across wheat fields to the nearest village.
STEVEN	Bloody hell. What do you do for milk?
WENDY	Buy long life?
MARCUS	There's a milkman.
STEVEN	A milkman?
WENDY	I thought they'd all gone extinct years ago.
COLIN	No, we've a milkman. He delivers.
MARCUS	Bread, eggs, cheese, butter...
COLIN	The daily essentials.
JAMIE	Is he attractive, this milkman?
COLIN	Old.
JAMIE	Pity.
WENDY	No shops, no pub, I don't know, it's a different world, isn't it, the countryside?
STEVEN	Middle of nowhere.
WENDY	Yes, it is.

MARCUS   We do have a car, though, don't we, Colin?

COLIN   Yes. I drive.

MARCUS   Yes, Colin drives. He drive to the train station every day. Colin commutes into work.

COLIN   London. Well, someone's got to pay the bills for this place, haven't they?

MARCUS   What does that mean?

COLIN   Nothing.

(*Colin drinks*)

WENDY   (*Drinks*) Oh, I love this wine. Fruity.

STEVEN   Yes, fruity.

JAMIE   It's what we drank on holiday last year, Steven, on the cruise, isn't it?

STEVEN   Is it?

JAMIE   Don't you remember, Steven? The night we met Colin and Marcus. We shared a bottle together.

(*Steven sips*)

STEVEN   Did we?

COLIN   Yes, we did.

JAMIE	Told you. It was my favourite, Col. Expensive, mind.

(*Colin pours Jamie more wine*)

COLIN	Have some more.
JAMIE	Cheers, mate.
COLIN	Cheers.

(*They drink. Colin pours himself another glass. Marcus watches Colin*)

MARCUS	Finished your glass already, Colin?
COLIN	Yes.

(*PAUSE*)

STEVEN	What are you drinking, Marcus?
MARCUS	Sparkling water.
STEVEN	Water?
MARCUS	I don't drink, Steven.
WENDY	You don't drink?
MARCUS	No. I haven't drunk for some months now, have I?
COLIN	No, he hasn't.
WENDY	Why not, Marcus? Don't you like the taste of it, wine?

21

MARCUS   I like the taste of it too much, I'm afraid, don't I, Colin?

COLIN   Yes, you do.

WENDY   Do you?

MARCUS   I did, yes, until I gave up. (*Sips water*) Colin's supposed to be giving up, too, aren't you?

COLIN   Yes. Eventually.

MARCUS   When?

(*PAUSE*)

WENDY   Oh, clean living, healthy boys are we?

COLIN   I wouldn't say that.

WENDY   Is that why you gave up London - too many temptations?

MARCUS   No, not really. I don't think so. Well... perhaps a few. Yes.

WENDY   Oh, and what were they?

MARCUS   (*Waves finger, joking*) Never you mind.

(*They laugh*)

STEVEN   Congratulations. Takes determination, does that, when a person gives up something, doesn't it?

MARCUS	Yes, it does.
WENDY	Oh, it does. (*Drinks*) I wish I could give up something. I can't give up anything. I've tried. I'm an addict. Chocolate, shopping, ciggies and booze, you name it, I like it. I've tried the patches, chewing gum, hypnosis, and nothing works. I'm a complete failure where addiction is concerned. A sad case.
STEVEN	Jamie gave up smoking last month, didn't you?
JAMIE	I did.
STEVEN	Nasty habit. Do you still smoke, Colin?
MARCUS	Yes he does, don't you?
COLIN	Yes I do.
WENDY	What about you, Marcus?
MARCUS	No, I don't smoke. Never have.
STEVEN	Don't drink, don't smoke, what do you do, Marcus? You must get up to something untoward?
COLIN	No, he doesn't. Almost a nun. (*Marcus looks at Colin, annoyed*) Only joking.
WENDY	(*She sips wine*) Very wise, never smoking. I've a chesty cough most mornings, haven't I, Steven?

STEVEN	Have you?
WENDY	Yes, first thing in the mornings I'm thick with catarrh. Cough my guts up, I do.
STEVEN	Something to look forward to on the cruise, boys.

(*Steven laughs. Wendy does not. Jamie looks around room*)

(*A series of paintings hangs on the wall. Different primary colours - red, green, blue, yellow*)

JAMIE	I like the paintings. Are these yours, Col?
COLIN	Yes.
JAMIE	Nice. (*Looks*) Do you like them, Steven?
STEVEN	(*Looks*) Interesting.
WENDY	(*Looks*) Yes, aren't they? Different.
COLIN	Thanks.

(*PAUSE*)

WENDY	(*Looks down*) I like your carpets, too.
MARCUS	John Lewis.
WENDY	Expensive looking, aren't they? A lovely pile, don't you think, Steven?
STEVEN	Yes. Luxurious.
WENDY	Makes you want to take your shoes off or something, doesn't it, wiggle your toes?

24

COLIN	Feel free.
WENDY	Saucy. Don't put ideas into my head, eh, Steven?

(*She laughs*)

COLIN	Oatmeal.
MARCUS	Biscuit.
COLIN	It's not.
MARCUS	It is.
COLIN	I thought we'd gone for the oatmeal.
MARCUS	Burnt biscuit.

(*Everybody looks at the carpet*)

COLIN	Really?
MARCUS	Yes.

(*PAUSE*)

WENDY	Well, I like it, whatever it is. Don't you, Steven?
STEVEN	(*Slightly irritated*) Yes. I've just said, haven't I?
WENDY	Jamie, do you?
JAMIE	Let me see.

(*Jamie smiles provocatively. Looks at Colin and Marcus. He takes off his shoes*)

STEVEN   What are you doing?

(*Jamie places shoes on floor. Slowly rubs feet on carpet, softly*)

JAMIE   Oh yes. I like it. Gorgeous. Luxurious.

STEVEN   What's he like, boys? An attention seeker, aren't you?

WENDY   Exhibitionist.

JAMIE   (*Smiles*) I might be.

STEVEN   Nice socks. Don't you think, lads? Jamie's socks.

(*Jamie raises a foot. Points leg out slowly. Arched foot [like a ballet dancer]*)

JAMIE   Purple silk, mate.

STEVEN   Yes. (*Steven lifts up the hem of his trousers. Steven wears the same purple socks*) Dolce and Gabbana.

(*Wendy seems slightly uneasy. Jamie smiles at Colin and Marcus. He sits. Wendy stands and looks out of the window. She turns back into the room*)

WENDY   (*Annoyed*) I could do with a new carpet. I keep meaning to treat myself. I say to myself every New Year, Wendy, next Spring it's paint those walls and chuck everything out. Start afresh. New carpet, new sofa, new life... the works. I never get around to it, though, do I, Steven...? I don't know why, do you, Steven?

STEVEN   Stuck in the past.

WENDY   (*Annoyed*) Am I?

(*Wendy sits. Picks up handbag. Looks into handbag. Continues to search in handbag*)

STEVEN   What are you doing, Wendy? She's always fiddling about. Aren't you?

WENDY   I can't find my lighter.   It's hiding somewhere. (*She looks*) Oh, here it is... (*She takes out cigarette*) Do you mind?   Is it allowed?   Smoking?

MARCUS   Where?

WENDY   In here. (*PAUSE*) I'll go outside, shall I?

COLIN   I usually do.

MARCUS   If you wouldn't mind.

WENDY   Right. Rules is rules. I'll smoke outside, then. I know my place, don't I, Steven? (*PAUSE*) Is it safe.

STEVEN   Is what safe?

WENDY   Outside.

27

STEVEN	Of course it's bloody safe. (*Laughs*) She sees danger in bloody everything, don't you, Wendy?
WENDY	Of course I do. It's the best way to survive in this world, isn't it? Where do I go? Where do you want me?
MARCUS	You'll find the garden through there.
WENDY	Righto.
COLIN	I'll show you the way, shall I?
WENDY	No, I'm fine. I'll find it. You stay here and do whatever you do. I know my place.

(*She stands. Annoyed*)

	I said when they telephoned, they should have said I was coming. It's only polite. I wouldn't like it, showing up with someone unannounced. Especially a... woman. I knew I'd be in the way.
STEVEN	What are you talking about?
WENDY	I said they should know I was coming.
STEVEN	What is there to know?
WENDY	I'm just trying to be au fait with this situation.
MARCUS	What situation?

WENDY	I don't know the procedure, do I, Steven, if nobody tells me? I don't know what to do. I can't always read the signals.
STEVEN	What signals?
WENDY	I'll be outside having my ciggie when you want me. Give me a shout when you've finished.
STEVEN	Finished what?
WENDY	(*Annoyed*) Oh, come off it, Steven. Jamie's had his shoes off stroking the carpet with his feet and you've been showing off your socks. Do you think I was born yesterday?

(*She goes*)

MARCUS	What's Wendy going on about?
JAMIE	Cock.
COLIN	Cock?
JAMIE	Yes.
STEVEN	She thinks that's what gay men want, all the time, when they get together. She thinks she's in the way a bit. She thinks we've been giving off some kind of... gay code.
MARCUS	Really?
JAMIE	Yes. (*Sips wine*) Cock.

29

(*Music. A long, sharp, searing note. glass-like/angel-like. Piercing*)

(*BLACKOUT*)

SCENE FOUR

(*Jamie stands looking at paintings on wall. Colin sits. Pours himself more wine. Drinks. Empties crisps into bowl. Places them on table. Far away, in the distance, a church bell tolls softly*)

(*SILENCE*)

JAMIE   Are you religious, Col?

COLIN   Why?

JAMIE   These paintings, they seem religious to me. Spiritual, like.

COLIN   They're just colours.

JAMIE   The colours seem religious.

COLIN   It's just a hobby. You see what you need to see, Jamie, don't you?

(*Jamie continues to look at paintings*)

JAMIE   Do you? (*PAUSE*) I don't know a thing about art.

COLIN   Me neither.

JAMIE   I like this one, the red one, what is it?

COLIN   I've no idea.

JAMIE   And the green?

COLIN   I don't know.

31

JAMIE   What about the blue? (*Colin shrugs*) You must do, if you painted it.

COLIN   I don't. I do it when I'm out of it.

JAMIE   Really?

COLIN   Yes.

(*Colin drinks*)

JAMIE   Why?

COLIN   Inspiration, I suppose. Detachment.

JAMIE   Detachment?

COLIN   Yes.

JAMIE   What's that, mate?

COLIN   It's when you need to disappear (*Sips*) from the so called real world.

JAMIE   I thought you liked it, living here?

(*PAUSE*)

COLIN   I do.

JAMIE   Like it, do you, getting out of it?

(*Colin says nothing*)

(PAUSE)

(*Smiles*)

	Me too. Good, innit? (*Jamie turns to look at painting*) How long have you been painting?
COLIN	Not long. (*Drinks*) I used to paint at school; a long time ago.
JAMIE	How much is this one worth?
COLIN	It's not for sale. I don't show them to anyone. It's just something I do. For myself. Personal.
JAMIE	Spiritual? (*PAUSE*) In the hospital where I work, giving out sandwiches and cups of tea, the patients in the psychiatric wing, some of them paint. Some of them paint like this.
COLIN	Thanks.
JAMIE	Have you ever had a breakdown, mate?
COLIN	Pardon?
(*PAUSE*)	
JAMIE	(*Smiles*) I'm forward, aren't I? Steven says I'm too forward. (*PAUSE*) I like this one. I think this painting, it's...
COLIN	What?
JAMIE	I don't know. What's it called?
COLIN	Nothing.

JAMIE	What you mean, nothing? (*He looks*) Well?
COLIN	It's called... (*PAUSE*) Well... it's... the feeling of... I'm not sure... what I call it.
JAMIE	Yes, you do. I think you do?
(*PAUSE*)	
COLIN	Do I?
JAMIE	Why's it called that, Col?
(*PAUSE*)	
COLIN	What? Love?
JAMIE	Yes. (*Smiles*) Got you there, didn't I? Tricked you into that one, didn't I? Revealed yourself there, didn't you? (*Jamie looks at Colin*) You don't like to give too much away, do you, Col?
COLIN	Don't I?
JAMIE	No. I like that. (*PAUSE*) Deep. (*PAUSE*) (*Jamie drinks*) You're both very artistic, aren't you, you and Marcus? We saw his film on television at Christmas – Mister Wispy. We saw his name come up on that kid's channel. We said, we know him, we've met the screenwriter, Marcus, on a cruise. We've had him. Very impressive.
COLIN	You should tell him. He'll be pleased.

JAMIE	What about?
COLIN	His writing.
JAMIE	He should write for Dr. Who. Writing for Dr. Who would be good. Lots of people watch Dr. Who, Casualty, Eastenders. Nobody watches... Mister Wispy. Well... only the under-fives, I would imagine.
COLIN	I'll bear that in mind, next time his agent rings. (*Sips*)
JAMIE	Has Marcus got an agent?
COLIN	Yes.
JAMIE	How fabulous. I wish I had an agent.
COLIN	What for?
JAMIE	Everything. (*Sips*) I'm going to be famous
COLIN	Doing what?
JAMIE	Nothing. Just being me. (*Jamie eats a crisp*) It's gone very quick, hasn't it, Col, since we first met, last year? Don't know where the time's gone, do you?
COLIN	No, not really.
JAMIE	I liked your emails. Dirty. (*PAUSE*) I thought I'd be living in New York or somewhere glamorous by now.

35

COLIN	There's still time.
JAMIE	Before I get old?
COLIN	You're not old, Jamie, you've years yet. You can do anything with your life.
JAMIE	Thanks. I intend to.

(*PAUSE*)

I'd best put these crisps down. I won't get into my new Boss suit. I'm still a twenty eight inch waist, mate.

COLIN	Congratulations.
JAMIE	Thanks. I work at it. Starve myself to death from time to time, but it's worth it, don't you think? Being boyish?

(*Colin looks at him*)

COLIN	Yes.
JAMIE	Thanks.

(*PAUSE*)

I like your aftershave, mate. What is it?

COLIN	Givenchy Gentleman.
JAMIE	Fresh.
COLIN	Thank you.
JAMIE	Mine's Chanel. "Allure".

(He holds out his wrist. Colin tentatively inhales Jamie's wrist)

(Wind chimes blow softly)

(Steven enters. Watches Colin and Jamie. A moment. Jamie turns. Looks at Steven. Winks. Jamie takes away his wrist from Colin)

	How is she, Stevie? How's Wendy?
STEVEN	She's fine. Still outside smoking.
JAMIE	Is she not coming back in?
STEVEN	She will do, eventually. She's looking up into the stars; like Bette Davis. She's being maudlin, but thinks she's being poetic.
JAMIE	How sad.

(Steven sits)

STEVEN	I see you two are getting on?
JAMIE	Yes.
COLIN	Have a crisp, Steven.

(Colin hands crisps bowl to Steven. Sits)

STEVEN	Thanks, I'm starving, we didn't stop, did we? We didn't eat on the way.
JAMIE	No.

(Steven eats crisp)

STEVEN   Perhaps we should send out for a takeaway.
                An Indian? A Chinese? What do you think?

JAMIE   That would be nice.

STEVEN   What do you think, Col? A takeaway for
                afters.

COLIN   Afters? After what...?

(*Steven smiles*)

(*PAUSE*)

                Marcus is rustling you up something, I
                think. A snack.

STEVEN   Right.

(*Steven eats a crisp*)

                What flavour are these?

JAMIE   Chicken.

(*Steven winks at him*)

(*Jamie drinks*)

                It's the drink, Steven. That's the problem
                with Wendy. She was at it in the Rolls.
                Sneaky nips.

STEVEN   Yes, she was. I could see her through my
                driving mirror. Whisky and gins in her
                handbag. Miniatures. She's fooling no-one.

38

JAMIE   Sneaky nips. I saw her.

STEVEN   Precisely. Women are moody buggers, aren't they, sometimes, Colin?

(*Colin drinks. No reply*)

JAMIE   She is. I can take my shoes off where I like, can't I, Steven?

STEVEN   Of course. There's no law against it, is there, Col?

(*Jamie looks at Colin. Jamie slowly strokes the carpet with his feet, sensually*)

(*Smiles*)

What's he like. Colin? A show off, eh?

(*Smiles*)

Little tart.

(*Jamie smiles*)

JAMIE   I might be.

(*SILENCE*)

(*Marcus enters with a tray of party food*)

MARCUS   Party nibbles. Here we are. A light supper. I've been through the freezer and found what I can. I'm sorry there isn't anything more.

39

JAMIE	Oh, party nibbles, thank you.
MARCUS	(*Smiles*) Help yourselves.
STEVEN	Much obliged. Mini sausage rolls, Jamie.
JAMIE	Nice one.

(*Steven takes some food off tray*)

MARCUS	I've told Wendy there's food, but she won't come in. Says she's on a diet.
STEVEN	She always is.
JAMIE	Don't know why. Like a stick insect.
STEVEN	You're still very slim, aren't you, Marcus?
MARCUS	I try.
STEVEN	Try? There's nothing of you, is there, Jamie?
JAMIE	Doesn't look like it.

(*Jamie takes some food off tray*)

MARCUS	Thank you. I'm still a thirty two inch waist, actually, Steven.
COLIN	He thinks he's fat, don't you?
MARCUS	(*Looks at Colin*) I do not.
STEVEN	Fat? Get away. Where's the fat? I can't see any fat. Can you, Jamie?

JAMIE	Not from over here. No, I can't.
COLIN	What did I tell you?
(*Colin drinks*)	
	He thinks he's got a belly. Can you believe it?
MARCUS	Shush.
STEVEN	A belly?
MARCUS	I do not. Shush.
STEVEN	(*Chuckles*) A belly? Where? I don't see any belly.
(*PAUSE*)	
	Show me.
(*PAUSE*)	
MARCUS	No.
(*PAUSE*)	
	It's hiding.
COLIN	Can you hear what they're saying?
MARCUS	Yes.
COLIN	You've no belly.
MARCUS	Good.

STEVEN	There was no belly last year on the cruise, was there, Jamie?
JAMIE	Nope.
STEVEN	Not in those Speedos.

(*PAUSE*)

Skimpy.

(*Colin pours more wine. Steven smiles at Marcus. Marcus looks slightly uneasy. Smiles back*)

(*Steven Eats*)

	It was a great time last year, wasn't it, lads? Ten days Mediterranean, Barcelona to Rome. A great cruise. The four of us, together.
JAMIE	Hot.
STEVEN	Yes, we often look at last year's photographs, don't we, Jamie? There's a nice one of you, Colin.
MARCUS	Is there?
COLIN	Where?
STEVEN	In the gym. Good pair of legs, hasn't he, Marcus?
MARCUS	Yes, he has. I've always liked Colin's legs. Masculine.

42

COLIN	Thank you.
MARCUS	Well, you are. I mean it.
JAMIE	I love a man's muscles, I do. Do you still wax, Col?
COLIN	Yes.
JAMIE	Good. Steven's started doing it, haven't you?
STEVEN	Yes. Makes everything much more defined.

(*To Marcus and Colin*)

Doesn't it?

JAMIE	Attractive. Younger.
STEVEN	Neater.

(*Steven looks around room*)

I must say, it all works in here doesn't it, the colour schemes, the fabrics, your little arty knick knacks. They all match, don't they? That's what you can do when you've been together some time, Jamie, make it feel homely.

COLIN	We try.
STEVEN	Our place is a mish mash. The docklands apartment. Nothing quite fits. A lot of styles going on.

43

JAMIE	Uncoordinated. I've told you, Steven. He's no taste.
STEVEN	(*Annoyed*) Really? (*Sips*) Did you get an interior designer in?
COLIN	No, we did it ourselves. Marcus is good at it.
MARCUS	It's having the confidence to experiment, isn't it, I find.
STEVEN	Oh, it is.
JAMIE	I couldn't do it, living here, the countryside. I couldn't do it, give up London. We still like to party and all that, don't we, Steven?
STEVEN	Oh yes, we do. I'm still very much a party animal.
JAMIE	Night prowling queens, we are. We're not ready to give up anything yet.
MARCUS	We haven't given up anything, Jamie.
JAMIE	Haven't you?
MARCUS	No, we don't live here because we've given up. We live here because we choose to. If you can live together without the need of outside stimulation, that's a good thing, isn't it?

JAMIE	Is it?
MARCUS	Yes, it is. Isn't it, Colin?
COLIN	Yes, if you can do it.
MARCUS	We do do it.
(PAUSE)	
COLIN	Yes, we do.
MARCUS	We moved away from London because we didn't need it anymore, the gay scene. It's empty. Feeding off itself all the time. We didn't give anything up. This was our choice.
COLIN	Yes, it was.
STEVEN	Good for you. At a certain age, if you know what you want, go for it, that's what I say. "The Old (*Looks around room*) Reading Rooms", I like it.
COLIN	Reading Room, Steven.
STEVEN	What?
MARCUS	It's called the Old Reading Room, this place, where we live.
STEVEN	That's what I said.
COLIN	No, you said the Old Reading Rooms, Steven.

45

STEVEN	Did I? What's your point? I don't get your point?
MARCUS	It's called the Old Reading Room, that's the point.
JAMIE	There's no "s", Steven.
STEVEN	Really?

(*PAUSE*)

	Does it matter?
MARCUS	Well, yes. Details. Everything is in the detail, don't you think?

(*Marcus sips water*)

STEVEN	I stand corrected.
JAMIE	Why's it called that, Colin, this house?
STEVEN	Cottage.
JAMIE	Why's it called the Old Reading Room, Col?
COLIN	Well... it was built by the church over two hundred years ago, you see. A priest taught people to read in here, peasants probably, people who worked on the land.
JAMIE	Oh? And why's that?
MARCUS	Why's what?

JAMIE	Why did he teach them to read? The peasants?
MARCUS	Knowledge, I presume.
JAMIE	Knowledge about what?
MARCUS	The Bible.
JAMIE	The Bible?
COLIN	Yes.
JAMIE	What for?
MARCUS	He wanted to save them, I suppose.
JAMIE	Save them?
COLIN	Yes.
JAMIE	Who from?
MARCUS	Themselves.
JAMIE	That's a bit condescending, isn't it?
STEVEN	I bet the peasants would have preferred a pub.
JAMIE	Probably.
STEVEN	Or a Wagamama.
JAMIE	Poundland.
STEVEN	Poundstretcher.

(*Steven and Jamie laugh*)

JAMIE   Dunkin' Donuts.

(*They continue to laugh. Marcus and Colin watch them. The laughter fades*)

(*PAUSE*)

(*SILENCE*)

(*Jamie stands. He walks about room, knowingly. Smiles. Crosses himself. Genuflects*)

STEVEN   What are you doing?

JAMIE   I'm being holy. (*Smiles innocently*) I went to Sunday School when I was little. I gave it up once I discovered Kylie Minogue and high heel shoes. From the age of nine... I preferred to show off my bare smooth legs.

(*PAUSE*)

He probably stood here, didn't he, all those years ago. The sexy priest... like this, and said... in the beginning there was the dark... and then there was... light.

STEVEN   What are you talking about? Sacrilegious, isn't he? Daft as a brush.

(*Jamie crosses himself*)

JAMIE   Once upon a time I was pure, Steven. Like us all.

48

(*Jamie looks at everyone. He winks*)

STEVEN   What's he like?

(*Jamie sits*)

Little tart.

(*PAUSE*)

Still... a stunner, though, isn't he? An excuse for anything, lads.

(*The wind chimes sound gently outside*)

(*SILENCE*)

COLIN   We couldn't believe it when we bought it, could we, Marcus, this place... It took a long time to find... but if a thing is meant... it's meant, I think.

MARCUS   Yes.

STEVEN   Good things always come to those who wait. What have I told you, Jamie? I always tell him that, every time he wants something, don't I?

JAMIE   You're just tight, Stevie.

STEVEN   As tight as your new Prada shoes. Two hundred and fifty pounds they cost me. Do you like them? Show 'em.

(*Jamie holds up one of his shoes*)

49

JAMIE	Black suede.
STEVEN	They make him look nice and expensive, don't you think?
JAMIE	I am expensive, Steven. Very.
STEVEN	They make him seem nice and looked after, don't they? Kept.
JAMIE	Almost.
STEVEN	He's never satisfied, are you?
JAMIE	Why should I be? I'm young, Stevie. (*Smiles*) You can try them on if you like.
COLIN	Sorry?
JAMIE	My shoes.
MARCUS	Why?
STEVEN	Go on. Slip them on. Have a go.
(*PAUSE*)	
MARCUS	No thanks. We're... fine.
JAMIE	Come on, Colin. What about you?
COLIN	I don't think...
JAMIE	I bet they suit you.
COLIN	No, Jamie, I'm fine.

JAMIE   Come on, try them. Slip them on. Let me do
                   it for you, Colin. Here. May I?

(*Jamie kneels. Undoes Colin's shoe*)

COLIN   (*Slightly embarrassed*) What you doing?

JAMIE   Relax.

(*Colin looks at Marcus. Marcus isn't sure what to say*)

(*Jamie eases off Colin's shoes. Puts a black suede shoe onto
Colin's foot. They all watch*)

(*SILENCE*)

(*Smiles*)

                   What do you think? Does it fit?

COLIN   It fits, yes.

JAMIE   Not too tight?

COLIN   No.

JAMIE   Snug?

(*Colin nods*)

STEVEN   Try the other one.

COLIN   No, I'm fine.

JAMIE   Go on.

COLIN   No, I'm fine. Honestly.

STEVEN	What about you, Marcus? Do you want to try it, the other one?
MARCUS	I'll pass, thanks.

(*Jamie eases shoe off Colin's foot. He sits*)

JAMIE	I like the feel of expensive things, don't I, Stevie? I love it.
STEVEN	Yes you do. And so do I. (*Drinks*) I like him to look good. Drives them jealous in the clubs, the other... gents. What do you think to his new hair-do, lads, Jamie's new image? What do you call it, Jamie, your new haircut?
JAMIE	I don't know.
STEVEN	Yes you do. (*Steven touches Jamie's hair*) Cost me sixty quid, did this. Look at the movement in it. Show them, Jamie.
JAMIE	No.
STEVEN	Show them the movement in it. Shake it, your haircut, go on, shake it.
JAMIE	No.
STEVEN	Go on.
JAMIE	Why?
STEVEN	I know you want to.

JAMIE	I don't.
STEVEN	Liar. Go on, we want to see. We like it, don't we, boys? Show us...
JAMIE	I'll spoil it, Steven.
STEVEN	Do it.

(*Jamie shakes head, flicks fringe*)

	See? See the movement? Marvellous, don't you think? Sexy.
JAMIE	Boyish.
STEVEN	It is. Don't you think so, lads? Makes you look a lot younger, Jamie, that fringe.
JAMIE	I'm not old, Steven.
STEVEN	I never said you were.
JAMIE	I'm seventeen.
STEVEN	Eighteen.
JAMIE	I'm not old, Steven.
STEVEN	Nobody said you were. He's just the correct age; not too young and not too old. In his prime, isn't he? For anything. (*He drinks*) Stomach as flat as the Norfolk Broads. Show 'em.
JAMIE	No.

STEVEN	Why not?
JAMIE	Because...
STEVEN	Sometimes he becomes all shy, don't you? God, I like that. Shyness. Gets me going. (*Smiles*) Pretty little thing. Vulnerable.

(*Outside, the wind chimes blow softly*)

(*SILENCE*)

MARCUS	Does anybody want any more crisps?
STEVEN	No thanks.
MARCUS	Are you sure?
STEVEN	I'm sure. (*He drinks*) I've lost five pounds since Christmas. Like you, Marcus, I don't want to get fat. I'm being careful. There's nothing worse than a belly, is there, hanging over a pair of jeans or a towel, whatever the age. Fat is fat. On a man or a woman. Fat is... a no-no. We see some fat sights in the sauna, don't we, Jamie?
JAMIE	Yes, we do, unfortunately.
STEVEN	Have you heard of the Equmen, Marcus?
MARCUS	Equmen? No, what's that, Steven?
JAMIE	It's a corset.
MARCUS	A corset?

STEVEN	Yes, it's like a vest, a sort of roll-on, a man's roll-on. It's for the belly, a man's midriff. It's American. It's not cheap, mind, costs about seventy pounds. It's all the talk at the Spartacus.
COLIN	Spartacus?
JAMIE	Steven's sauna franchise.
STEVEN	Yes, I've got my own sauna business. Men only. If you get my drift. (*Drinks*) You want to make a note of it, Marcus.
MARCUS	Sorry?
STEVEN	The male corset. It's been reviewed in all the magazines - Attitude, GQ, Sunday Times Magazine. The Equmen holds everything together like a tight fitting skin. An undergarment. It comes in three colours, white, blue, and black. It works very well. A meshy material. A tight stretch nylon. According to the reviews and word of mouth, it's marvellous. A miracle. Like a rubber band.
JAMIE	(*Unimpressed*) Tesco's are doing one. A cheaper version, of course. Aren't they, Steven?
STEVEN	Yes. I'm told that's very good too. It doesn't ride up or anything, even while dancing. You want to make a note of it,

Marcus. Should you be bothered about a belly, buy yourself an Equmen vest.

MARCUS   Thanks for the advice, Steven. I'll bear that in mind.

STEVEN   Don't mention it.

(*Marcus seems slightly offended. Colin notices*)

COLIN   You don't need one, Marcus. A...

MARCUS   (*ANNOYED*) Don't I?

COLIN   No, of course not.

(*Marcus reaches for a crisp. He eats crisp*)

Honest.

MARCUS   Thanks.

JAMIE   (*Innocently*) When you're wearing one, Marcus, you can't tell. Nobody knows the difference. The problem is, when you take it off. Then you've a problem, haven't you, Steven? When you take it off and everything is revealed, you can knock someone sick.

STEVEN   How would I bloody know? (*Drinks*) Still, who cares as long as you've got hold of them where you like... eh, lads... tight, in bed. (*Suddenly Steven puts his arm around Jamie's neck. Holds him in a lock. A grip*)

(*To Colin and Marcus*) Eh, lads?

JAMIE   That's selfish, Steven.

(*Steven lets go of Jamie*)

STEVEN   (*Smiles*) So what? A pickup can't escape once you've got him. Locked away where you want him. You've won, haven't you?

JAMIE   Yes. If you're only after sex. (*Jamie drinks*) Some people are after more, though, aren't they?

STEVEN   Are they?

(*PAUSE*)

COLIN   Yes.

(*Music. A long, sharp, searing note. Glass-like/angel-like. Piercing*)

(*BLACKOUT*)

SCENE FIVE

(*Marcus sits. Colin stands pouring wine*)

MARCUS   (*Annoyed*) The sarcastic queen.

COLIN   He didn't mean you, Marcus.

MARCUS   Yes he bloody did. The insulting trollop.

COLIN   Hush. He'll hear you.

MARCUS   I don't care. I don't care what Steven bloody hears.

COLIN   He wasn't referring to you personally. He didn't mean anything by it. He was talking generally. Trust me, you don't need a corset.

MARCUS   I know I bloody don't. How dare they draw attention to my appearance? (*Looks into the mirror. Starts checking himself*) You know I don't like it, my body, at the best of times.

COLIN   Your body's fine, for your age.

MARCUS   I beg your pardon?

COLIN   You haven't got a belly, Marcus.

MARCUS   (*Annoyed*) I know I bloody haven't.

COLIN   So let's just drop it, shall we?

MARCUS   Then why did you mention it?

58

COLIN	I didn't. They did. They were just... trying to be helpful, I suppose.
MARCUS	Helpful? What was helpful about it?
COLIN	Stop getting so uptight, will you.
MARCUS	You haven't been criticised, Colin.
COLIN	They were just trying to relax you, that's all. Trying to make you feel better about yourself. Getting you going.
MARCUS	Getting me going? What are you talking about, Colin?
COLIN	They were trying to get you going, weren't they, sexually? They're after a bit, aren't they?
MARCUS	They've got a funny way of going about it, haven't they? A fuckin' corset.
COLIN	Hush, will you?
MARCUS	No I won't. I want them to go. We moved away from London so we wouldn't have to meet people like this anymore. Scene queens. I loathe them.

(*Colin drinks*)

COLIN	Don't whine, Marcus.
MARCUS	I'm not whining, Colin, I'm expressing myself. I want them to go.

COLIN	They're not staying long
MARCUS	How do you know?
COLIN	They said they're just breaking up their journey.
MARCUS	And bringing a woman with them, too. I can't believe it, can you? The cheek. The liberty.
COLIN	You liked them last year on the cruise.
MARCUS	Last year I was drunk. You shouldn't have given them our email, Colin. I blame you.
COLIN	You told me to.
MARCUS	I did not. When?
COLIN	The night we did it with them. The four of us.
MARCUS	(*Closes his eyes*) Well I'm not doing it with them now. I'm not getting up to anything like that with them in here. (*Marcus opens eyes*) Our home.
COLIN	I'm not asking you to, am I?
MARCUS	Good.
COLIN	You're always touchy nowadays, aren't you, Marcus?
MARCUS	I am not.

60

COLIN	Yes you are. You spend too much time analysing everything.
MARCUS	So? I've had a lot on my mind, Colin, haven't I, recently, thinking about my writing. Mister Wispy. I've a mental block.
COLIN	You've had a mental block for nine months.
MARCUS	So?
COLIN	Long enough to have a baby.
MARCUS	Fuck off. (*Annoyed*) Being creative, Colin, isn't easy, especially when you don't feel good about yourself. It brings on my low self-esteem.
COLIN	Again.
MARCUS	Yes, again. And when you don't feel good about yourself, you don't want to take your clothes off for anyone, including you, and especially for them. Every time I look in the mirror, all I can see is my body's faults, the saggy bits, and your going on at me all the time, well, it doesn't help.
COLIN	(*Annoyed*) Look, sometimes Marcus, you need to get lost inside. Sometimes you need to let yourself go.
MARCUS	Don't start.

COLIN	Sometimes I need to go there with you. I need to do that with you. It's a ritual. One of the last rituals left, isn't it? That's why people, governments, try to control it, isn't it? Sex. It's the only time, the only real time, people can be free, isn't it? And I want to be free with you. I want that spell... that mystical act with you. Fucking.
MARCUS	Hush.
COLIN	I want it with you. Fucking. Belly or no belly.
MARCUS	Will you hush.
COLIN	Fucking. Fucking. Fucking.
MARCUS	(*Annoyed*) Hush. Someone will hear you.
COLIN	Tough.

(*Colin drinks. Marcus watches him*)

MARCUS	How many drinks have you had?
COLIN	The same as everyone else.
MARCUS	And how many is that?
COLIN	A few.
MARCUS	Liar.
COLIN	We've got guests, haven't we?
MARCUS	So you've already said. Any excuse.

(*Colin drinks. Pours himself another glass*)

Did you like wearing his shoe?

(*PAUSE*)

COLIN   What do you think?

MARCUS   Steven's showing him off like a first prize trophy.

COLIN   ...Jamie bait.

MARCUS   Yes. They're both terrible, aren't they? Blatant. Outrageous.

COLIN   He's got a cute smile, though, hasn't he? Angelic. A nice kid.

(*Marcus looks at him*)

What you doing?

MARCUS   I'm looking at your eyes.

COLIN   Why?

MARCUS   I want to see.

COLIN   Why?

MARCUS   You know why, Colin.

COLIN   Give over. Fuck off.

MARCUS   I want to see.

COLIN   No.

MARCUS   Colin.

(*Colin looks at Marcus. They stare into each other's eyes*)

COLIN   Satisfied?

MARCUS   No, not really. (*PAUSE*) You've taken something, haven't you? You're on something, aren't you?

COLIN   No.

MARCUS   You are.

COLIN   No I'm not.

MARCUS   Have you taken something more than drink?

COLIN   No. What's the matter with you?

MARCUS   You know what's the matter? How much have you taken?

COLIN   Everything's fine. I'm fine this evening. Honest. (*PAUSE*) Stop worrying. I've stopped. You know I have. Come here.

MARCUS   No.

COLIN   Please.

MARCUS   No.

(*PAUSE*)

(*Marcus goes and sits next to Colin*)

COLIN	Thank you. (*Colin leans over to Marcus. He kisses him on the cheek, tenderly*) There. (*PAUSE*) See?
MARCUS	When we moved, you promised you'd stop everything, and...
COLIN	I have.

(*Marcus looks at him*)

Honest. I've taken nothing.

(*PAUSE*)

MARCUS	(*Smiles*) You smell nice.
COLIN	It's new.
MARCUS	What is it?
COLIN	Givenchy Gentleman.
MARCUS	Nice. When did you buy it?
COLIN	Last week.
MARCUS	You never said.
COLIN	Boots.
MARCUS	Did you put it on because of them?
COLIN	What?
MARCUS	Did you put it on because you knew they were both coming?

COLIN	No. I put it on because I like it.
MARCUS	You never told me.
COLIN	Told you what?
MARCUS	That you bought it.
COLIN	I don't have to tell you everything I do, do I?
MARCUS	Yes.
COLIN	Why?
MARCUS	Because. (*PAUSE*) Boots?
COLIN	Yes.

(*PAUSE*)

MARCUS	Where was I? I never saw you buy it.
COLIN	You were there.
MARCUS	What was I doing?
COLIN	Buying your mouthwash, and tweezers.
MARCUS	Givenchy Gentleman?
COLIN	Yes.

(*Colin holds out his wrist. Marcus inhales Colin's wrist*)

MARCUS	Nice. (*Looks at him*) Sexy.

COLIN   Good. Thank you. (*Smiles*) I asked you last
               year if you liked it. You said no. You said it
               was too musky. I tried it on in Debenhams.
               Christmas Eve.

MARCUS   I don't recall.

COLIN   You were in one of your moods. Some
               assistant made a joke about the pom poms
               on your hat and you told her to keep her
               rude remarks to herself. It was just after
               you stopped drinking. She called you a
               pixie.

MARCUS   Really?

COLIN   Yes. A pixie.

MARCUS   Really?

COLIN   Yes.

MARCUS   That doesn't sound like me, does it? A
               pixie?

COLIN   No? (*PAUSE*) A narky pixie, yes.

(*Smiles. They look at each other*)

MARCUS   You won't spoil things, will you, Colin? Not
               again. You won't spoil things ever again,
               will you? Promise? (*PAUSE*) I can never
               feel safe. (*PAUSE*) I need to feel safe.

(*Outside, far away, the wind chimes blow gently*)

(*Colin and Marcus, hand in hand, sit in silence. A tenderness*)

COLIN   I'm fine. Everything's fine. We're both fine. I promise. No more worries.

(*Wendy appears at door. She watches them, slightly uneasy*)

WENDY   Hello.

COLIN   Oh, hello.

MARCUS   Enjoyed your smoke?

WENDY   No, not really, I've ran out. (*PAUSE*) What you both doing?

MARCUS   Holding hands.

WENDY   Oh? (*PAUSE*) Am I in the way?

COLIN   No, you're not in the way, Wendy. Come on in. Sit down.

WENDY   Are you sure? Because I've been in the way before, where Steven is concerned. He doesn't tell me what he's up to, you see, until I usually twig it, and then sometimes it's too late.

MARCUS   You're not in the way, Wendy. Have a vol au vent.

WENDY   Are you sure?

COLIN   Yes, sit yourself down.

WENDY   Righto. But only if you're sure.

68

(*She picks up a vol au vent*)

MARCUS   I can wrap them up for you if you like.

WENDY   Why?

MARCUS   For when you're going.

WENDY   Are we going? Has Steven said?

MARCUS   No, not yet

WENDY   (*Sighs*) Right. (*She sits*) Jamie's in the garden, smoking. Steven will go mad if he sees him. Where is he?

COLIN   Who?

WENDY   Steven.

MARCUS   Toilet.

WENDY   Right. (*PAUSE*) Have you a few ciggies I can cadge, Colin, I've ran out.

COLIN   Yes, in my suit pocket. I'll fetch them, shall I?

WENDY   If you wouldn't mind.

(*Colin leaves. He's slightly unsteady for a moment. He steadies himself. Marcus, concerned, watches him. Colin leaves*)

Colin likes a drink, doesn't he?

MARCUS   Does he?

WENDY	Yes, it's an alcoholic country here in Britain, isn't it?
MARCUS	Is it?
WENDY	Oh yes. Where I live everyone wees in the street, every night. Not just at the weekends. Standards have dropped, haven't they? Girls just kneel down without any knickers and squat. The lads get an eyeful, and nobody seems to care. Where's the dignity? What would Queen Victoria say?
MARCUS	She'd be shocked, I expect.
WENDY	Oh, she would, because I have to squirt around my front door with disinfectant, constantly. (*She eats vol au vent*) Has he been up there long, Steven, in the toilet?
MARCUS	Actually, yes, he has.
WENDY	What's he doing?
MARCUS	Toilet, I hope.
WENDY	Nowadays he tends to take his time. He's best left to it, I find, however long it takes. I don't interfere. The last time I timed him it was nearly half an hour.
MARCUS	Half an hour?
WENDY	Yes, on the toilet.

70

MARCUS	Why?
WENDY	I never ask. He gets too touchy. (*PAUSE*) He's got a hernia, you see. Two. One each side, here and there, from lifting weights, I believe. He needs to go a lot when he drinks. Pressure. (*Drinks*) Still, you've got to laugh, haven't you?
MARCUS	What about?
WENDY	Middle age. Its peculiarities. The ups and downs. (*Wendy stands, picks up a small pork pie*) May I?
MARCUS	Yes, of course.
WENDY	Thanks, I'm famished. Bang goes my diet. (*Eats*) Are you not eating, love?
MARCUS	No, I'm watching my figure, too.
WENDY	Very wise. It's very body conscious, the gay scene, isn't it? You gays are very vain, aren't you? Very body conscious. Very judging.
MARCUS	Are we?
WENDY	God, yes. You don't want to get a belly, do you?
MARCUS	(*Put out*) No.

WENDY	(*She peers out into garden, through window*) The light's slowly vanishing. Beautiful out there this evening, isn't it? Have you seen? (*PAUSE*) The twilight. (*PAUSE*) Magical. (*She eats*) Hey, don't let on to Steven, will you? About what I've just said? He says I've got a runaway tongue. He doesn't like me talking about his personal health issues; not where his sex life is concerned. Touchy. (*Eats*)
MARCUS	There's nothing going on, Wendy - not like that - not in here. Things of a sexual nature I mean.
WENDY	Isn't there?
MARCUS	No.
WENDY	Are you sure?
MARCUS	'Course I'm sure.
WENDY	You can tell me. I'm very broad minded.
MARCUS	There's nothing going on.
WENDY	(*Sighs*) I believe you. (*She doesn't*) (*Wendy peers out of window again. Turns back*) That Jamie better hurry up. Steven doesn't know. He thinks Jamie's given up smoking, but he hasn't. It's mine and Jamie's secret. One of many, I might add. And not the last, I expect. (*She looks outside again, through*

72

window) There's so many stars out there, isn't there? Up in the sky, they're all coming out. Layers upon layers. So many stars up there. All the dead people. You'd forget if you didn't look up... the heavens... all hidden away. (*PAUSE*) (*She sighs, looks at watch*) What time is it in Turkey, do you think?

MARCUS   Turkey?

WENDY   Yes. What time is it? Do you know?

MARCUS   No. Why do you ask?

WENDY   No reason. (*She looks out of window again*) We're all governed by the stars, aren't we? Our destinies. The future. What star sign are you?

MARCUS   Pisces.

WENDY   (*Looks at him*) Really? So am I. We're the same, aren't we? We've got something in common, haven't we?

MARCUS   Have we?

WENDY   We're both needy, aren't we?

MARCUS   Are we?

WENDY   Yes, I think so. I can feel it. I can tell. I'm like that. I sense things. Tender things. (*She pours herself a drink. Marcus watches,*

73

slightly put out) (*PAUSE*) What sign's Colin?

MARCUS Taurus.

WENDY Oh, the bull, that makes sense.

MARCUS Why?

WENDY Sexy, isn't he?

MARCUS I think so.

WENDY Who wouldn't.

(*PAUSE*)

MARCUS Thank you.

WENDY (*PAUSE*) Yes, Jamie's supposed to have given up. I don't know how he'll manage when we're away, stuck on a ship. Steven's bound to find out. I'm surprised he hasn't twigged, but Steven's like that where Jamie's concerned. He turns a blind eye to lots of things. Only sees what he wants to see. Still, we're all like that in some ways, I suppose, aren't we? Hiding the truth. Pretending.

MARCUS Are we?

WENDY Yes. I think so. (*She sits*) (*Outside, the wind chimes are heard*) (*SILENCE*) Did you know Steven had been married?

74

MARCUS	No, I didn't. He's never said.
WENDY	Oh yes. Steven was married for nearly twenty years. We got a divorce about...
MARCUS	You?
WENDY	Yes, me and Steven... must be ten years ago now. He said enough was enough... Once the truth was out, well... what's the alternative? You can't play at a marriage, can you? Not mine, anyway. (*PAUSE*) No more babies for me. (*PAUSE*) I think he's happier being a homosexual, do you? A gay. (*Drinks*) I can live with it. We still get on. People can accept most things nowadays, as long as you're not hurting anybody. It's prevalent everywhere, different lifestyles, isn't it? The soaps are full of it. Muslim this, gay that, wheelchair access everywhere. You've got to be tolerant. It's the best way, isn't it, keeping your mouth shut? (*Looks out of window*) (*Softly*) I love the twilight. (*PAUSE*) Isn't it quiet here? (*PAUSE*) You forget what it's like, don't you, living with no noise. Where I live, I'm surrounded by noise all the time. Thump, thump, thump. Other people's music. Does my head in. Everyone making themselves known. Here, it's... peace and quiet... all around you... like a

church... the quiet of... a church... A sacred place. Here, you can get to know yourself.

(*SILENCE*)

We need it, peace and quiet, sometimes, don't we? The silence. A purity. (*PAUSE*) Without it we'd go mad.

MARCUS   Yes. (*Far away, the wind chimes blow outside*)

WENDY   Oh, that's lovely, isn't it? A lovely sound. What are the wind chimes for, exactly? Are they just ornamental, or... do they signify anything in particular?

MARCUS   They're Chinese. They keep away the ghosts, the dark spirits.

WENDY   Really? Do you believe in things like that, other worlds?

MARCUS   Yes.

WENDY   Why?

MARCUS   I just do. Living with Colin... I...

WENDY   What?

MARCUS   (*Softly*) Nothing.

WENDY   Do you believe in God, Marcus? I believe in God. What else is there if you need to feel wanted? I've found nothing else lately,

76

anyroad. You've got to believe in something, haven't you? (*PAUSE*) You've been together a long time, haven't you?

MARCUS   Yes, we have.

WENDY   I can tell. It's your mannerisms. They go together, don't they? A lot of gay men have that in common, don't they? You all look the same. The same person, I mean. Safety in numbers, I suppose.

MARCUS   Pardon?

WENDY   How long have you been together, Marcus?

MARCUS   Twenty years.

WENDY   Twenty years?

MARCUS   Yes.

WENDY   A lot longer than some marriages.

MARCUS   Yes.

WENDY   Longer than mine, anyroad.

MARCUS   Yes.

WENDY   That's love I suppose, isn't it?

MARCUS   Yes.

(*Wendy drinks*)

WENDY   Do you know what I think, Marcus? Nobody does anything for anyone because of love, they do it out of a need. A need for something in themselves. (*PAUSE*) A hole. A cut. A wound. (*PAUSE*) Don't you think? Deep down inside, we're all sliced open. Weeping.

(*SILENCE*)

Oh, where is everybody? Isn't it quiet? It's very quiet, isn't it? I don't like it. You notice the quiet, don't you, especially when talking... with yourself.

(*SILENCE*)

(*A toilet flushes*)

Oh, here he is. Here he comes. Lord and master.

(*SILENCE*)

(*Steven enters. Stands at door. His mood changed. Tense. Angry. But keeping it together, hidden inside*)

(*A stillness*)

(*Wendy looks at Steven*)

What's up with you, stranger? What you been doing? Up to something, I bet. What you been up to?

(*Steven enters room. Says nothing. He sits. Marcus watches him*)

(*SILENCE*)

(*The mood of the room has changed. The light getting darker*)

STEVEN   Can I have a whisky, Marcus?

MARCUS   A whisky?

STEVEN   Yes.

(*PAUSE*)

MARCUS   I'm not sure we have any, Steven.

(*PAUSE*)

WENDY   Hasn't it gone dark, don't you think, Steven, outside?

(*PAUSE*)

STEVEN   Would you check, please. I'd like something that burns.

MARCUS   Burns?

STEVEN   The back of my throat. A whisky. With ice.

MARCUS   I don't think we...

STEVEN   (*Sudden anger*) Would you check... (*PAUSE*) (*Softly. Controls anger*) Please.

MARCUS   (*Slightly disturbed at Steven's outburst*) Yes.

79

(*PAUSE*)

(*Marcus leaves. Wendy looks at Steven*)

WENDY What's up with you, Steven? What's... the matter?

(*SILENCE*)

(*Steven closes his eyes*)

(*Far away a church bell tolls softly*)

(*Wendy stands. Looks out of window*)

(*SILENCE*)

It's lovely out there, don't you think? Did you look from upstairs into the garden? It's a beautiful night, isn't it, Steven? Magical. (*PAUSE*) The twilight. (*PAUSE*) Dusk.

(*She looks at Steven. He opens his eyes. He looks at her*)

(*SILENCE*)

STEVEN (*Softly/violently/slowly*) Fuckin' shut it.

(*Music. A long, sharp, searing note. Glass-like/angel-like. Piercing*)

(*BLACKOUT*)

END OF ACT 1

ACT 2 SCENE ONE

(*Moonlight through the window*)

(*Steven eats crisps slowly. One after the other, from bowl. Tense. Brooding*)

(*A clock chimes*)

(*Wendy watches him. Steven knows he's being watched by Wendy. He is uncomfortable. Inside, he is slowly seething. A stillness. Anger, but controlled*)

(*SILENCE*)

(*Eventually:*)

STEVEN   (*Seething/irritable*) What are you staring at, Wendy?

WENDY   I dread to think. (*PAUSE*) What's the matter, Steven? What's upset you? (*She sips*) 'Cos whatever's the matter with you, don't take it out on me. Understand?

STEVEN   (*Daring her*) Take it out?

WENDY   Yes.

STEVEN   Take what out?

WENDY   (*Drinks*) Look, it's not my fault, is it? You can't blame me for anything, not this time. I told you when you got involved with him, I said...

81

STEVEN   (*Looks at her [seething]*) Don't go there,
                  Wendy, don't bloody go there. If you know
                  what's good for you, don't...

WENDY   Right. (*Knocks back drink*) Are we off,
                  then? Because I need to get booked into
                  that hotel, sharpish. I want to relax, use the
                  facilities, and put my hair in heated rollers.

STEVEN   Hang it up, more like.

WENDY   Sarcastic sod, aren't you, at times, when
                  you're pissed off with someone?

STEVEN   Am I?

WENDY   Yes.

(*They both sit in silence, looking out front, both their faces
emotionless, like masks*)

                  (*Softly*) I care for you, Steven.

STEVEN   (*PAUSE*) Aren't I the lucky one?

WENDY   (*Annoyed*) Yes you bloody are, considering.
                  (*Wendy turns to look at Steven*) Are you sure
                  you're alright?

STEVEN   Yes, I'm alright, Wendy.

(*PAUSE*)

WENDY   No problems? Upstairs.

(*PAUSE*)

STEVEN	What?

(*PAUSE*)

WENDY	The toilet.
STEVEN	The toilet? Why should there be a problem?
WENDY	No reason. Just askin'. You took your time, that's all.
STEVEN	Were you timing me again?
WENDY	No, of course not. I was just wondering what you were doing; whether you... saw?

(*Marcus enters*)

MARCUS	There we are, Steven - one scotch with ice.
STEVEN	Thank you.

(*Steven takes glass of whisky. Drinks. A hard swig. Wendy and Marcus watch. Steven hands glass back to Marcus. A tenseness*)

	Much obliged. Might I have another? One for the road?
MARCUS	Oh, you're going, are you? You're off?
STEVEN	Soon.
WENDY	Yes. Past Jamie's bedtime, isn't it?
STEVEN	(*Irritated*) Another drink, Marcus, please.

83

WENDY   Another drink, Steven? Is that wise if you're driving?

STEVEN   (*Annoyed*) Hasn't stopped me before, has it?

WENDY   Nothing stops you, Steven. Unfortunately.

MARCUS   Right. (*Marcus switches on lamps in room*) (*PAUSE*) (*Feigned smile*) One whisky with ice.

STEVEN   (*Feigned smile*) Please.

MARCUS   Righto.

(*Marcus leaves*)

(*SILENCE*)

WENDY   So, come on then, tell me, did you see anything outside, from the bathroom window?

(*PAUSE*)

(*Steven seethes*)

STEVEN   (*Daring her*) See what?

WENDY   You know what. (*Sarcastically*) The cows?

STEVEN   (*Annoyed*) Cows?

WENDY   (*Goading him*) Yes. They've got cows. Did you notice from the bathroom window? They've got cows. (*PAUSE*) Moo moos.

84

(*PAUSE*) You can hear them in the dark, back field… munching.

(*Steven silently seethes*)

STEVEN   Munching?

WENDY   Yes. (*She calls*) There's a bull, too, isn't there, Marcus, outside.

MARCUS   (*Calls*) Yes. A prime beef Angus.

WENDY   (*To Steven*) See. It all happens in the countryside, doesn't it, in the dark? (*She seems to be goading Steven*) Munch munch munch.

STEVEN   (*Irritated*) How much have you been drinking?

WENDY   Not enough, darling. (*She opens handbag. Takes out a pill. Swigs it with drink*) Down the hole.

(*Jamie enters*)

JAMIE   Hiya.

WENDY   Oh, here he is. (*Smiles*) Little Prince Charming. Isn't he gorgeous? Butter wouldn't melt in his mouth, or anywhere else, would it, Steven?

(*Jamie stands innocently looking at them both*)

JAMIE   What's up with you two?

85

STEVEN	(*Coldly*) Where have you been?
JAMIE	(*Smiles*) Fresh air.
WENDY	Did you see them, Jamie? Bottom of the garden?
JAMIE	See what?
WENDY	The cows.
STEVEN	Shut up, Wendy.
JAMIE	Yes, I did.
WENDY	Munch munch munch.

(*Jamie sits*)

JAMIE	What you going on about?
WENDY	You. (*She drinks*)

(*Marcus enters with glass of scotch*)

MARCUS	Here we are, Steven. Another scotch. Last drop, I'm afraid.

(*Steven takes glass*)

STEVEN	Thank you.

(*Marcus sits*)

MARCUS	Where's Colin?

(*Steven drinks. Watches Jamie*)

JAMIE	In the garden having a smoke.
WENDY	Very nice out there, isn't it? The garden.
JAMIE	Awesome. Went on forever.
STEVEN	What did?
(*PAUSE*)	
JAMIE	The countryside.
STEVEN	Are you chewing?
JAMIE	No.
STEVEN	Liar. He's always chewing. He looks like a bloody cow himself when he's chewing. Spit it out.
JAMIE	What?
STEVEN	I don't like it.
JAMIE	So.
STEVEN	Spit it out.
JAMIE	Why should I?
STEVEN	Because I said so. I've told you I don't like it, constant chewing.
JAMIE	Who cares?
STEVEN	I care.
JAMIE	What's got into you all of a sudden?

STEVEN	(*Annoyed*) I said stop your chewing.
JAMIE	And I said, no?
STEVEN	(*Annoyed*) Spit it out.
MARCUS	(*Slightly taken aback*) Really. All this... behaviour... it's...
JAMIE	You're embarrassing me.
STEVEN	Do it, I said.

(*Jamie takes out chewing gum from mouth*)

JAMIE	Satisfied?

(*Wendy opens handbag. Takes out tissue. Holds tissue out. Jamie places chewing gum in tissue. She places tissue in handbag. Shuts handbag*)

MARCUS	Is something the matter, Steven...? I feel... there's...
WENDY	Nasty habit, chewing, isn't it? Like smoking.
STEVEN	(*Looks at Jamie*) Filthy.

(*Colin enters. He seems drunker. More out of it. Carrying a tray of drinks*)

WENDY	Oh look, here he comes, the dreamboat.
MARCUS	Where did you find that lot?
COLIN	(*Drunker*) Under the sink. Why?

88

MARCUS   Why?

COLIN   Your ciggies, Wendy.

(*Hands them to Wendy. He puts tray down*)

WENDY   Thanks, love.

(*Colin pours himself a drink. Everybody looks at him*)

COLIN   What's up?

JAMIE   (*To Steven, innocently*) Nothing.

STEVEN   Oh, isn't there?

(*Steven is looking at Colin, angrily/threateningly. Wendy doesn't like it. Wendy suddenly sniffs the air, 3 times [quickly], changing the subject*)

What's the bloody matter with you? Like a bloody rabbit.

WENDY   Can I smell something?

COLIN   Sorry?

WENDY   Chips? Is somebody cooking?

MARCUS   Cooking? Yes, somebody is. Colin is. Aren't you?

COLIN   Me? Am I? (*Thinks*) I am not.

MARCUS   Oh yes you are. (*To everyone*) He always does this when he's... drinking. He does things and then he forgets things, don't you?

COLIN   Do I?

MARCUS   Yes, you do. All the time.

(*PAUSE*)

COLIN   What did I forget this time, Marcus?

MARCUS   You put the cooker on, left some chips in the oven, and went away. McCain's. Rustic French Fries.

COLIN   McCain's? Rustic?

MARCUS   ...French Fries, yes.

(*PAUSE*)

JAMIE   I like chips.

COLIN   When did I do that, then - the chips?

MARCUS   I don't know. When you went for Wendy's cigarettes, I presume.

COLIN   Shite. (*Rubs face*) I don't remember.

MARCUS   No, of course you don't

JAMIE   Are we having chips, mate? I'd like some chips, Col, if there's any going.

STEVEN   Well you can't have any.

JAMIE   Why not?

90

STEVEN   (*Firmly*) Because we're going and I said so.

JAMIE   Really? (*Annoyed*) Well... get you.

(*Steven looks at Jamie, annoyed*) (*SILENCE*)

STEVEN   (*Feigned smile*) He's a headcase, isn't he? (*Looks back to Colin*) Don't you think so, Colin? Jamie, always playing daft? Jamie likes to play silly buggers sometimes, don't you? Tries to wind me up.

COLIN   Really? (*Steven pours himself wine*)

STEVEN   (*To Jamie*) Yes, he does.

WENDY   That's naughty, Jamie, isn't it?

STEVEN   Yes, it is. (*Sips*) Very naughty. (*Looks at Jamie*) Dangerous, too.

MARCUS   (*Looks at Jamie, then Colin*) You took your time, didn't you, going for those cigarettes? What else have you been doing?

COLIN   I was in the toilet.

STEVEN   Jamie said you were in the garden. (*Steven drinks*)

COLIN   I was, having a smoke, wasn't I?

JAMIE   Yes.

COLIN   (*Looks at Marcus*) Why?

(*Marcus sips water, annoyed*)

91

MARCUS   Nothing.

(*SILENCE*)

(*They drink*)

STEVEN   (*Sits*) He'd be good for you, actually, Colin,
                    wouldn't he, Jamie, don't you think? A
                    good case study to sort out.

COLIN   How do you mean, Steven?

STEVEN   (*To Wendy*) Colin sorts people out, don't
                    you? Their funny ways.

COLIN   I try to.

STEVEN   Colin's a Social Worker in London, Wendy.

WENDY   Oh? Really? How interesting.

(*They drink*)

JAMIE   Could I have some tomato sauce, Marcus?

MARCUS   Tomato sauce?

JAMIE   On my chips?

MARCUS   I think Steven said you're not allowed.
                    You're going soon, Jamie, aren't you?

JAMIE   I'm hungry, Steven. Please, let Jamie have
                    some chips... (*PAUSE*)

(*Steven looks away*)

A few chips won't hurt him, will it?
(*Boyishly*) Please.

(*Steven looks at Jamie. Steven's eyes reveal a tenderness that he cannot hide*)

WENDY   (*Watches*) You're too soft on him, Steven.

(*PAUSE*)

JAMIE   Please, Stevie, chips? Please. (*PAUSE*)

(*Steven sighs. Nods*)

STEVEN   (*Softly*) Very well.

(*PAUSE*)

JAMIE   (*Smiles*) Thank you, Stevie.

(*Wendy is not pleased. Drinks*)

Chips, Marcus.

(*Marcus looks at Steven*)

MARCUS   (*Annoyed. Sighs*) Anyone else?

STEVEN   No ta.

WENDY   No thanks.

MARCUS   (*Annoyed*) Colin?

COLIN   What?

MARCUS   Chips?

COLIN   Chips?

MARCUS   (*Annoyed*) Rightio.

(*He goes*)

(*Steven, Jamie, Wendy, sit alone with Colin, Colin's eyes closing*)

(*SILENCE*)

WENDY   What kind of people do you sort out, Colin, in your job? London?

COLIN   Eh? (*Thinks*) Oh, drug addicts, petty criminals usually. I mainly listen to lots of their excuses, the reasons why they haven't turned up in court. Boring really.

JAMIE   Yes, he hates it, don't you, mate? Commuting into London every day, listening to crap.

COLIN   Somebody's got to do it, Jamie. It pays the bills.

(*Marcus appears at door*)

MARCUS   And what do you mean by that? (*Then turns to Jamie*) Salt and vinegar?

JAMIE   No thanks.

MARCUS   (*To Colin*) Because I go to my shed, Colin. Remember? I write all day. Remember?

(*Marcus leaves.*)

COLIN   (*Calls*) I never said you didn't.

MARCUS   (*Calls*) Good. Just because I don't have any paying commissions at the moment, doesn't mean to say I don't work.

COLIN   (*Calls*) I know you work.

MARCUS   (*Calls*) I'm working on Mister Wispy, aren't I? Part 2. For myself, at the moment. (*PAUSE*) Expressing myself. (*PAUSE*) Artistically.

COLIN   (*CALLS*) Good. I know.

(*SILENCE*)

(*They sit in silence, the four of them looking at each other. Weighing each other up for some time*)

(*The wind chimes blow gently outside*)

(*Marcus enters with a bowl of French fries with tomato sauce on them. He holds a fork*)

MARCUS   (*Feigned smile*) Rustic French Fries, Jamie.

(*He hands the bowl of chips to Jamie*)

JAMIE   Thanks. How very kind.

MARCUS   One tries.

(*Looks at Colin*)

(*Jamie begins to eat chips. Looks at Steven. Winks. Steven winks back. Wendy is not pleased. She tuts*)

COLIN   Where do you work, Wendy?

WENDY   On a till, love. It's not very interesting.

STEVEN   It's a job. Somebody's got to do it.

WENDY   I wish I didn't. (*Sighs*) Aldi. It was never my dream, until after my divorce, then it became a necessity.

MARCUS   Did you know Steven and Wendy were married, Colin?

COLIN   No. Really?

WENDY   (*Drinks*) Oh yes. A church wedding. Picture in the paper. Fairytale do, everything.

COLIN   Fancy.

WENDY   Yes. I thought my life was charmed forever, didn't I, Steven? (*PAUSE*) We had a son, too, didn't we? Tony. But he died, though, didn't he, Steven? Our little boy.

(*PAUSE*)

STEVEN   Yes.

(*PAUSE*)

JAMIE	Nice chips, mate. Well cooked. Want one, Steven?
STEVEN	No thank you. I've already said, haven't I?
JAMIE	Go on. Try one. (*PAUSE*) Shall I blow on it for you?
STEVEN	No. Behave.

(*Jamie continues to eat, then takes hold of a chip with his fingers. Looks at chip. Slowly blows on the tip of the chip. Jamie looks at Steven. Jamie goes to Steven. Moves the chip to Steven's mouth. Steven looks at Jamie. Slowly opens his mouth. Jamie pops the chip into Steven's mouth. Jamie smiles. Steven eats*)

JAMIE	Very tasty, don't you think?
STEVEN	Yes. Tasty.

(*Jamie sits. Jamie continues to eat chips*)

JAMIE	You were saying, Wendy.
WENDY	(*Angry*) I was saying, it was a big wedding. Big cake. Big train. Big bouquet. The works. (*PAUSE*) Once upon a time.
COLIN	How interesting.
MARCUS	You never said, Steven, did you, you were married?

(*Steven looks at Colin and Marcus [unimpressed]. Says nothing. He drinks*)

STEVEN   So?

WENDY   He never does, do you? I'm his dirty secret, boys.

STEVEN   (*Annoyed*) I don't need to tell anyone, Wendy, do I? She tells everybody I meet, eventually.

WENDY   (*Drinks*) It happened, didn't it?

STEVEN   It most certainly did.

(*A clock chimes. Marcus looks at watch*)

MARCUS   It's getting very late, don't you think? what time do you sail in the morning?

STEVEN   Five o'clock.

MARCUS   You're going to be very tired, aren't you?

STEVEN   We sail at five o'clock in the evening, Marcus.

MARCUS   (*Slightly disappointed*) Oh, right.

JAMIE   (*Continues to eat chips*) Are they attractive, mate?

COLIN   Who?

JAMIE   The petty criminals you sort out.

COLIN   Some.

JAMIE   Tattoos?

COLIN	Some.
JAMIE	Nice. I like the sound of that - drug addicts and tattoos. Don't you, Steven? Men pierced. I'm into that. I've told Steven to get his done.
WENDY	Get his what done?
STEVEN	Shut up will you.
JAMIE	Would you ever consider having yours done, Marcus?
MARCUS	My what?
STEVEN	Shut up, will you. Never stops, does he? Always at it.
WENDY	Yes, shut up, Jamie. Marcus and Colin don't want to hear about unhygienic things like that - do you? ...It's disgusting. (*Drinks*) Drugs are so prevalent nowadays, aren't they, Steven? It's terrible. I come across junkie's paraphernalia every time I open a dustbin. It's a disgrace.
JAMIE	You smoke.
WENDY	Pardon?
JAMIE	Benson and Hedges. Packets of them.
WENDY	So? What's that got to do with anything?
JAMIE	Nicotine's a drug, Wendy. And you drink.

WENDY	So what?
JAMIE	Double standards, that is, isn't it, Steven?
STEVEN	Leave her alone, will you. Stop playing with her.
JAMIE	What's got into you? Moody, aren't we?
STEVEN	Eat your chips and hurry up, so we can get off.
MARCUS	Shall I fetch your coats?
WENDY	I'm no druggie, Jamie.
JAMIE	You take pills. Temazepam. Handfuls
WENDY	Medically prescribed, for my nerves.
JAMIE	And she eats her diet pills, morning, noon, and night, don't you? Like M and M's.
STEVEN	She's not a druggie, Jamie. There's a big difference. She goes private.
WENDY	Yes. I'm medically approved. Legally provided for by Steven. Druggies are illegal. A nuisance to society. Aren't they, Steven?
STEVEN	Yes. They break into everyone's business. I've got bars on my sauna windows.
WENDY	(*Smiles*) Is that to keep the punters in or out, love?

STEVEN	(*Smiles*) Very funny.
JAMIE	We both do the odd line, though, don't we, Steven?
WENDY	The odd line?
JAMIE	Coke.
WENDY	Coke?
JAMIE	Charlie.
STEVEN	(*Annoyed at Jamie*) Shut up.
JAMIE	Drugs are only a problem if you can't handle them, Wendy, aren't they, Col?
COLIN	Sometimes.
MARCUS	No they're not. What are you talking about?
JAMIE	Drugs are...
MARCUS	Devastating.
JAMIE	No they're not.
STEVEN	(*To Jamie. Annoyed*) Be quiet, I said.
JAMIE	No, I won't. Chill, will you? What's up with you? Christ.
WENDY	I didn't know you sniffed coke, Steven. You never said.
STEVEN	I don't.

WENDY	When did that start? This habit?
STEVEN	It hasn't.
JAMIE	What's the big deal? Most people do it, don't they, Colin? Most people do the odd line while watching porn. So what?
WENDY	Porn? Do you? When did you start on that, Steven? You never told me.
STEVEN	It's nobody's bloody business, Wendy, is it?
WENDY	Do you like it, then, porn?
STEVEN	Porn is porn, Wendy. I can take it or leave it.
WENDY	Gay porn? You never said, Steven. You never told me.
STEVEN	I don't have to tell you anything, do I?
WENDY	What's it like, then, this gay porn? Is it more...? I bet it is. What about you, Colin, do you watch it, porn?
COLIN	Sometimes.
WENDY	Gay porn?
COLIN	What else would it be?
WENDY	What about you, Marcus? Do you indulge?
MARCUS	Indulge? How do you mean?

102

WENDY	Watching porn. Gay porn.
MARCUS	Well, it has been known, Wendy.
WENDY	Bloody hell, you're all at it. What's it like, then, gay porn? Would a woman like it?
MARCUS	I've no idea.
JAMIE	Depends on what sort it is.
WENDY	How do you mean? What sort do you watch, Steven?
STEVEN	Never you mind. Keep your nose out.
WENDY	Why? Go on, tell me. I want to know.
STEVEN	It's personal.
WENDY	Personal? We had a child together, didn't we? I've been with you sexually, Steven.
STEVEN	This is different. This is...
JAMIE	Male rape.
(*PAUSE*)	
WENDY	What?
STEVEN	Be quiet.
WENDY	(*Shocked*) Male rape? Christ, why do you want to watch that?
JAMIE	Power.

103

STEVEN	It's just a bit of...
WENDY	What? Jesus, I'm shocked... Jesus, Steven?
STEVEN	It's not real, is it? Don't cause a fuss. It's playing. It's just... men larking about. Fun. Fantasy. Entertainment. Isn't it, lads?
MARCUS	Keep me out of it, Steven, please.
WENDY	Entertainment? Rape?
MARCUS	Calm down, Wendy, please.
WENDY	I will not calm down. (*Drinks*) You men, what are you like? The things you get up to in the name of entertainment... Entertainment up the bum? What are you like? I've never heard the like. Entertainment?
STEVEN	Shut up.
WENDY	(*Shocked*) Actually, I have, heard about it, that's not true. This article in my magazine, "Chat", it said male rape is on the increase. It seems the horrendous things men do to women, they're doing it to themselves now. What's that all about, eh? I don't understand it. Would someone explain it to me please, the attraction, Marcus - rape, up the bum?
MARCUS	How should I know?

WENDY	Well, you're a man, aren't you?
MARCUS	Yes, but I'm not a bloody rapist, am I?
WENDY	How do you know?
MARCUS	Pardon?

(*Colin smiles. Laughs*)

	And what are you laughing at?
COLIN	Chance would be a fine thing, wouldn't it?
MARCUS	Oh, drink your drink and be quiet.
WENDY	All men are potential rapists, aren't they?
STEVEN	Where the hell did you get that idea from?
WENDY	The feminists in the 1970's.
STEVEN	Shut up.
MARCUS	Actually, Wendy, you're quite safe with me, because I've never been with a woman sexually. And...
WENDY	Haven't you?
MARCUS	No, never.
WENDY	Why not?
MARCUS	Why do you think?
COLIN	The vagina.

JAMIE	Yes, we don't go there, do we, Steven? Very squeamish about that, aren't we? Adamant. Not for us. Ever. Don't like them, do we? (*To the men*) Us boys.
WENDY	Well that's just another form of prejudice, isn't it?
STEVEN	Give over.
WENDY	(*Drinks*) (*Baffled*) What goes on in those minds of yours, men's minds. Come on, I'd like to know.
STEVEN	Ignore her. She's drunk.
WENDY	I'm not drunk. I'm tipsy. Come on, Colin, tell me, what goes on in men's minds?
COLIN	(*Drunker*) Well, nobody really understands the mind, do they, Wendy? Not even psychiatrists. There's still a lot to know, isn't there? A mystery.
WENDY	It bloody sounds like it. I've never heard the like of it, Steven... Entertainment? Up the bum? (*PAUSE*) Rape? Jesus Christ.
JAMIE	We probably didn't have to ask for it, once upon a time, did we? When we were animals we probably just did it, took whoever we wanted. The strongest could just do it, penetrate the animal it wanted, with no questions asked. Don't you think, Colin?

COLIN	I'm sure.
STEVEN	(*To Jamie*) Well, thank you, David Attenborough
JAMIE	It's just an opinion.
STEVEN	We're supposed to be having a pleasant evening, aren't we? All this talk of dirt... animals... bums... It's...
WENDY	Unholy. (*Sips*) I've never heard the like of it. Larking about? Fantasy? Up the bum? (*She drinks*) Gay or not gay, you've got to draw the line somewhere, haven't you? We were married, Steven. (*Wendy places down her empty glass*) Jesus.

(*PAUSE*)

COLIN	More wine, Wendy?
STEVEN	No, she doesn't. She's had enough.
MARCUS	Don't encourage her, will you? They need to get going, don't you?

(*Colin gives Wendy wine, slightly unsteady on his feet*)

COLIN	Here we are, Wendy.
MARCUS	I said don't encourage her. Do you hear, Colin?
WENDY	Are you trying to get me drunk, Colin? Anaesthetise me? After the shock?

107

(*Colin stands with his eyes slightly closing*)

Yes you are. Isn't he awful, Steven? How do you live with him, Marcus?

(*Flirts at Colin*)

The little devil.

(*Steven looks at Wendy and Colin, drunk*)

STEVEN   (*Drunk, himself*) Pathetic. (*To Marcus*) Aren't they? A pair.

MARCUS   How many bottles have you opened, Colin?

(*Colin doesn't reply. He continues to pour himself drink*)

Will you stop that?

STEVEN   Drunken bugger.

WENDY   (*To Colin*) You look like how I feel, love. I won't be able to get up in the morning. What must I look like?

STEVEN   (*Sarky*) A picture of health. Gorgeous.

WENDY   (*Sarky*) How would you know? (*Opens handbag. Takes out compact mirror. Looks at herself*) Oh, look at the state of me. Why didn't you tell me, Colin? What a fright.

COLIN   (*Drunk*) You look fine, Wendy.

WENDY   Flatterer. How do you put up with him, Marcus? He's a tease. (*Wendy applies* *lipstick. Looks at herself in mirror*) The mysterious Irish type aren't you, Colin? Deep, dark, and handsome. Go on then, tell me, as a man, how old would you say I look? Come on, tell me.

COLIN   (*Drunk*) I've no idea.

WENDY   Yes, you have. Come on Colin.

COLIN   What?

WENDY   How old do I look, sweetheart? For real.

COLIN   I don't know.

WENDY   Guess. Come on, don't be shy. I won't be offended if you get it wrong.

JAMIE   Yes she will.

WENDY   I won't. Come on, have a good guess. Marcus?

STEVEN   Leave them alone, will you? They don't want to guess. Can't you see they don't want to get involved with your... games.

WENDY   My what?

JAMIE   Insecurities.

WENDY   (*Becoming drunker*) Come on, have a good butchers'. Come on, Colin. Guess. How old am I? Man to woman. Take me in, look me up and down, all over, and... what do you think? (*She stands, hands on hips, sexually, giving Colin the big, powerful, female come-on*) Well?

(*Colin looks. He is slow, trying to slightly focus*)

COLIN   I'm not sure.

WENDY   It can't be that difficult, can it?

COLIN   Is she... Are you forty two?

(*Wendy looks closely at him. Wendy smiles at him [slightly more sexual]*)

JAMIE   And the rest.

(*Colin smiles at Wendy, drunk [slightly sexual]*)

COLIN   Forty five?

STEVEN   Higher.

COLIN   Forty eight?

WENDY   (*Sexual*) Lower.

COLIN   (*Sexual/playing*) Forty six?

STEVEN   Higher.

WENDY   Come on, Marcus, join in. Don't be shy. Come on, Babes.

MARCUS   (*Irritated*) Forty seven.

WENDY   Lower.

MARCUS	Forty three?
JAMIE	Higher.
COLIN	Sixty?
WENDY	Fuck off. Lower.
COLIN	Forty... something?
JAMIE	And the rest.
STEVEN	(*Irritated*) One hundred...
JAMIE	Higher.
STEVEN	One hundred and eighty.

(*Everybody laughs*)

WENDY	Bastards.
JAMIE	She's ancient.
WENDY	(*Hurt*) Give over.

(*They laugh*)

(*Annoyed*) Stop it. Stop it, will you. Stop it.

(*The laughter stops*)

MARCUS	Sorry, Wendy.
COLIN	Yes, sorry.
STEVEN	She's fifty.
WENDY	I'm not.

111

STEVEN	Fifty.
COLIN	Fifty?
STEVEN	Yes.
WENDY	You've spoilt it now, Steven. As usual.
COLIN	Are you? Fifty? Really?
WENDY	No I'm not, I'm forty nine.
STEVEN	Fifty.
JAMIE	Same age as my nan. When she died.
WENDY	(Annoyed) I'm forty nine. And proud of it.
STEVEN	You're fifty.
WENDY	Forty nine, Steven. And I don't want to argue. I'm not in the mood.
JAMIE	She disguises it well. Don't you? Her age. She spends a fortune on cosmetics, don't you?
WENDY	Yes, I do. Much more than food. How you look is how you feel. Nowadays, appearance is everything. (*Looks into mirror*) Still... forty nine, it's a strange one. I must admit... (*She applies lipstick. Smudged. Looks in mirror*) ...you can see a real change in the skin as you get older, can't you, Steven?

112

STEVEN	Can you?
JAMIE	Yes, you can.

(*Steven looks at Jamie*)

STEVEN	Well thanks a bunch, honey.
JAMIE	I didn't mean you, Steven. I meant...

(*He glances at Colin. Looks away*)

STEVEN	Christ, he's so transparent, isn't he?
WENDY	Don't start, boys. No arguments. No lovers' tiffs. Not in front of company.
JAMIE	I wasn't talking about your skin, Stevie.
STEVEN	And who's skin were you talking about? How many older men do you touch up?
JAMIE	None.
STEVEN	Liar. (*Looks at Colin, then back at Jamie*) I can see right through you, Jamie boy. I can see right through you like glass.
WENDY	Cut glass.

(*Colin slowly closes his eyes*)

	Is Colin not well?
MARCUS	He's fine.
COLIN	(*Opens eyes. Looks at Jamie/drunk*) I'm fine. (*Smiles at Jamie*) Aren't I?

113

STEVEN   You won't be fine when...

WENDY   (*Steps in*) Colin should eat something
                 properly, don't you think, Marcus, with all
                 this drinking? A lining on his stomach.
                 Haven't you got a Pot Noodle or
                 something?

MARCUS   Well... I...

COLIN   I'm not hungry, Wendy.

(*Colin's eyes drop*)

WENDY   Colin's been drinking a lot. Haven't you?
                 Far too much, darling.

(*Marcus nudges Colin*)

MARCUS   Will you wake up?

COLIN   (*Annoyed*) I'm fine. Cool it.

WENDY   Here, try these nibbles, they'll soak
                 everything up, love. Have one of these. A
                 cheese whatsit. (*She hands nibbles to Colin.
                 He takes one. Marcus takes one, too. They
                 both eat. Wendy stands looking at Colin and
                 Marcus*) Ah, don't they look nice, don't you
                 think, Steven? Together. (*Smiles*) Are you
                 both foodies? I bet you are, aren't you? Gay
                 foodies.

MARCUS   Gay foodies? No, I don't think so, are we,
                 Colin?

114

COLIN	Gay foodies? (*Drunk*) No. The last time we went to a restaurant was our wedding, wasn't it, Marcus?
MARCUS	Yes.
JAMIE	Wedding? (*To Colin*) You never said, mate.
COLIN	Four months ago. A small affair.
MARCUS	Intimate. Just the two of us.
COLIN	Yes.
WENDY	(*Drunk*) Oh, congratulations. A wedding, Steven. (*Drinks*) I noticed the rings on your fingers, but I didn't like to say anything. That's marvellous, isn't it? (*Looks at rings*) Oh, very nice. Have you seen, Jamie?

(*Jamie looks*)

JAMIE	Nice one.
STEVEN	Colin never said there was a wedding, did he, Jamie? No mention of that in his emails.
MARCUS	Emails? What emails?
WENDY	How romantic. A gay wedding.
STEVEN	You should have said. We would have brought you something if we'd known, wouldn't we?

WENDY	Yes. A white orchid or a box of La Maison du Chocolat. We usually do.
COLIN	It doesn't matter.
MARCUS	Yes it does. What emails have you been sending, Colin?
JAMIE	It was just friendly talk. Chit chat, mate. Nothing.
MARCUS	Nothing?
JAMIE	Nothing dirty. No pictures or anything. No Skype.
MARCUS	(*Annoyed*) Colin.
COLIN	What? (*Colin's eyes begin to close*)
MARCUS	(*Annoyed*) Wake up.
WENDY	Well I think it's wonderful. After such a long time together you're entitled to a wedding, aren't you? Do you feel any different now you've done it?
MARCUS	What? (*Looks at her, slightly confused*) Yes, I think so.
STEVEN	In what way?
MARCUS	Every way…
WENDY	More secure?
MARCUS	Well… yes.

116

COLIN	Yes.
WENDY	Good.
JAMIE	You don't need a ring on your finger to feel like that, Col, do you?

(*Colin looks at him [drunk]*)

I don't want to get married. I always want to feel that little bit different. Sexually. I don't feel the need for anybody else's approval. Actually, I feel I'm... superior. More advanced. I don't want to fit in, ever...

STEVEN	More advanced than who?
JAMIE	Heterosexuals. Homosexuals. I'm an advanced species. No labels.
STEVEN	Are you?
JAMIE	Yes, I am.
STEVEN	He reads magazines, don't you? He gets his ideas from magazines.
JAMIE	I like to be informed, Steven, that's all. Intellectually.
STEVEN	He reads these things and pretends they're his thoughts, don't you? He says these things, but he doesn't know what he thinks, do you?

117

JAMIE	Why get married? Why saddle yourself like you and her did?
WENDY	I beg your pardon?
JAMIE	Marriage didn't work for you, did it, Wendy?
WENDY	Only because my husband had a roving eye.
JAMIE	A gay one.
WENDY	Not at first.
JAMIE	And what does that mean?
WENDY	Everything. Steven loved me, didn't you, Steven? It wasn't just about sex when we made our son, Tony. Our little boy. It was the real thing. You loved me, didn't you Steven?
STEVEN	(*Uncomfortable*) Yes. I did. (*PAUSE*) ...I tried.
WENDY	What?
JAMIE	We're not supposed to stay together, are we, Col? A life forever with one person, it's mad, isn't it? Why bother? Why pretend? Clinging together out of fear. Animals don't pretend, do they?
COLIN	That's true. Survival of the fittest, with them.

118

MARCUS	(*Annoyed*) We got married because we wanted to, Jamie. Thousands of men campaigned for it, the freedom to choose, that's all.
JAMIE	Why bother?
COLIN	Equality.
WENDY	(*To Jamie*) Yes, so millions of boys like you can stick their arses in the air and flaunt it on a Mediterranean cruise.
STEVEN	Precisely. He's got no idea. His lot take everything for granted. They'd have gassed him once upon a time, wouldn't they, along with the gypsies, Jews, blacks and spastics.
WENDY	Yes, they would.
JAMIE	I'm not interested in the past. I'm only interested in now.
STEVEN	(*Annoyed*) Shut up.
JAMIE	Why be so dramatic? You always have to be so dramatic, Steven.
STEVEN	Shut up, I said. You haven't got a clue what you're talking about.
MARCUS	No, he hasn't.
JAMIE	We're having a conversation, aren't we?

STEVEN	Bloody shut up, I said. The brains of a little girl.
JAMIE	Can't we have an intelligent conversation together? (*Annoyed*) You're so dumb, Steven, sometimes, with your old fashioned views.
STEVEN	Oh, am I?
JAMIE	Yes. Thick.

(*Steven sits fuming. Tension*)

WENDY	What do you mean, Steven? What do you mean when you said you loved me... at least you tried.
STEVEN	Jesus. I didn't mean anything.
WENDY	Yes you did.
STEVEN	(*Annoyed*) Christ, you're always bringing it up. You're obsessed with it. Let it rest, will you?
WENDY	Obsessed with what?
STEVEN	Marriage.
WENDY	No I'm not.
STEVEN	Yes you are. You're always talking about it. Any chance she gets, she brings it up and drops it into the conversation.

WENDY	I do not.
MARCUS	(*Stands*) Can I have your glasses please. I think it's time I washed up.
WENDY	Saying your vows in public is everything, isn't it, Marcus. It brings meaning to something. A sacred act. Everything else is just fumbling about in the dark.
MARCUS	I agree.
COLIN	True.
WENDY	Good. (*To Steven*) Are you feeling guilty, Steven?
STEVEN	No, I'm bloody not. What about?
WENDY	Me.
STEVEN	(*Angry*) Of course I'm bloody not.
WENDY	Then why are you starting to lose your temper?
STEVEN	I'm not losing my temper.
WENDY	Yes you are. Isn't he, Marcus? I can read the signs.

(*Steven sucks in his breath*)

	See?
JAMIE	(Worried) Remain cool, Steven. Ignore her.

STEVEN   I am cool.

(*He blows out*)

JAMIE   Don't let her rile you.

MARCUS   (*Annoyed*) Your glasses, please.

WENDY   I'm riling no-one. I can't help it if you're riddled with guilt. Even his own mother won't talk to him, Marcus, not anymore. She says if she knew then what she knows now, Colin, she wouldn't have had him. She's from a different generation of course - old East End - but it's still upsetting for her, isn't it, Steven, your behaviour? Your selfishness. Turning gay. Choosing to... like...

(*Steven looks at Wendy, grinding teeth*)

Don't start. Now then.

(*Steven to himself, growls. Steven blows in and out for some time, clenching fists*)

Don't start. Stop that.

STEVEN   Stop what? (*Growls at Wendy. Clenched teeth*) Gertcha.

WENDY   Stop it Steven. I won't have it. Do you hear? You're not talking to your mongrel dog now.

122

JAMIE	You leave Mr Scruffy out of this.
STEVEN	(*Growls*) Gertcha.
MARCUS	What's he doing?
WENDY	I know what he's like when he starts. His temper.

(*Steven tries to control his temper*)

MARCUS	Would anyone like coffee?
COLIN	(*Drunk*) Yes please.
STEVEN	(*Annoyed*) She's a typical woman at times, isn't she?
WENDY	Am I?
STEVEN	Yes.
WENDY	And what's that?
JAMIE	A shit stirrer.
WENDY	Fuck off.
MARCUS	I think you all need to calm down, don't you?
COLIN	Yes.
WENDY	(*Annoyed*) Oh, do you?
MARCUS	Yes, just a little, Wendy. You're becoming a little destructive, don't you think? Tell them, Colin.

123

COLIN	Shush. (*Drunk*) Don't be bitchy, Wendy.
WENDY	Bitchy? (*Annoyed*) I thought you gays were supposed to like women?
COLIN	We do, don't we?
MARCUS	Yes, we do. (*Looks Wendy up and down*) Most of the time.
WENDY	Well, you've got a funny way of showing it, ganging up on me, because, sat here, right now, it's me who feels like I'm in the minority. And it's not right. I feel very isolated, I can tell you, and it's not very pleasant. I feel like I'm the outsider. The odd one out. (Wendy looks at her watch. Sighs.)
STEVEN	Don't start.
WENDY	(*She looks at watch*) What time is it in Turkey?
COLIN	Turkey?
WENDY	Yes.
MARCUS	What's the big thing about Turkey?
STEVEN	Jesus, she's off. It's started. Look, we don't want to hear about bloody Turkey. Do you hear me? Not now. Not in here.
JAMIE	Not ever.

WENDY	(*Pleased*) He's only jealous. Aren't you Steven?
STEVEN	Jealous? Am I? What of?
WENDY	Mustafa.
MARCUS	Mustafa?
COLIN	Who's Mustafa?
STEVEN	A Turk.
JAMIE	Wendy's new addiction, fling.
STEVEN	She sends him gifts in the post, don't you?
WENDY	Yes, I do.
JAMIE	Money.
STEVEN	Two thousand bloody pounds.
WENDY	Who's counting?
JAMIE	I am.
WENDY	Mustafa likes me a lot, Colin. And Steven can't stand it.
STEVEN	He's got a wife, Wendy.
WENDY	So what? It doesn't mean anything out there. They have to get married over there if they want sex. They're Muslims.
JAMIE	She believes everything he tells her.

125

STEVEN	Yes. (*To Wendy*) He saw you coming. Mother fuckin' Theresa.
WENDY	If you'd met him, Marcus, and you both knew him, Colin, you wouldn't say that.
COLIN	(*Drunk*) Wouldn't we?
STEVEN	I've seen his photograph. His gold tooth. That tells me enough.
WENDY	How racist. You're only jealous.
STEVEN	Jealous of what?
WENDY	I've got what you gays can't have. A man. A straight man.
MARCUS	I beg your pardon? What do you mean by that, Wendy?
STEVEN	Yes, bloody shut up, will you?
WENDY	Oh, I hear things about you, Steven, I'm not daft. People talk. I've heard about the complaints in your sauna. Those poor married men. The pestering that goes on under their cubicles. The bribing, with money. The stealing of undies. (*Steven looks at Jamie*)
JAMIE	I've told her nothing.

WENDY	Oh, haven't you? He tells me everything. He thinks it hurts me, don't you, rubbing my face in the shit?
JAMIE	Lying cow.
STEVEN	Don't rise to it, Jamie. You know what she's like when she starts. The spite. Keep cool.
JAMIE	Bitch.
WENDY	Queen.
JAMIE	That's homophobic, Wendy.
WENDY	Good. You pouffe.
JAMIE	Slag.
WENDY	Sissy boy.
MARCUS	(*Annoyed*) Oh, please. Really.
JAMIE	She's always been like this, since the day we met, after a drink, Marcus. Homophobic.
MARCUS	You are a bit, aren't you, Wendy. A little homophobic.
WENDY	(*Annoyed*) So what? I'm entitled. (*Shouts*) I married one, didn't I? A queer.
STEVEN	Right, that's it. I've heard enough.
MARCUS	And so have I. Can I have your glasses, please?

127

WENDY	No.
MARCUS	Colin, tell them.
COLIN	What?
STEVEN	There's nothing worse than a drunken woman, is there? Look at it.
WENDY	Fuck off.
MARCUS	(*Nudges Colin*) Colin.
COLIN	What?
MARCUS	Tell them I want them to go. Now.
COLIN	Later.

(*Colin nods, eyes closed*)

STEVEN	I apologise profusely for her behaviour, Marcus. I'm sorry about this. I apologise.
WENDY	(*Angry*) Well don't. (*Wendy opens handbag. Takes out a miniature bottle - gin. Wendy goes to window. Walks. Steadies herself. Looks outside*)

(*Outside, the wind chimes blow gently*)

(*SILENCE*)

Mustafa, he's a good one. Gentle and... attentive.

(*Swigs from miniature*)

128

STEVEN   (*Softly*) Jesus and Mary.

(*Wendy opens pill bottle. Takes out a pill. Swallows*)

WENDY   (*Turns to look at room*) I only went to Turkey by chance, didn't I? (*Drinks. Wendy stares at the blue painting called "Love"*) Another world... Sun behind his head, face in shadow. I was lying on the beach trying to forget everything when... (*She turns to look at them*)

JAMIE   (*Sarcastic*) "Coconut ice, madam?"

WENDY   It must have been about eighty two degrees. A clear blue light. And...

JAMIE   "Oh, I was thirsty..."

WENDY   Yes... coconut ice. They sell it to you like coca cola. Mustafa was standing in front of me. Dark brown eyes... a little down on his lip... soft... a tender tash... Funny, the things you remember. It made him seem... so... vulnerable. (*Softly. Tenderly*) Smiling. (*She smiles. Closes eyes*)

(*Outside, the wind chimes blow gently*)

He came back to see me on the same day, three times. Unusual spices on his skin. Exotic, tantalising, foreign.

(*Opens eyes*) I don't regret anything, Steven. Everybody should have a romantic story to tell sometimes, shouldn't they?

COLIN   (*Softly*) Yes.

STEVEN   (*Annoyed*) And that's all it is, a story. They have a different woman every day, those Turkish tikes. There's plane-loads of English old women going over to Turkey for a bit every day.

JAMIE   Cock.

STEVEN   Bronzed cock.

WENDY   Straight cock.

STEVEN   Paid for by me. My credit card.

WENDY   I don't care. I'm not ashamed. Whatever he wanted, he provided something for me, and I provided something for him. He liked me and I liked him. He loves women and you two can't stand it. I'm going to fly back and see him some more. I'm going to make love to him some more in the sun... again and again and again... (*Softly. Tenderly*) Fucking.

STEVEN   (*Disgusted*) Have you heard what you sound like? You're... a disgrace to your sex. Call yourself... a mother.

JAMIE	The randy mare.
STEVEN	She's paying for sex. A woman, paying... for sex.
WENDY	So what? (*To Steven*) You spend a fortune on lover boy here. Armani underpants, Dolce and Gabbana socks, the washing list is endless.
STEVEN	That's different.
WENDY	What's different about him?
STEVEN	We're a relationship.
WENDY	Oh please, is that what you call it? Oh please. (*Laughs*) Now who's deluding themselves? How very modern. (*Angry*) Well, see if I care.
JAMIE	You'll care in the morning, when you sober up.
STEVEN	Yes, she'll care when we get her on the Queen Mary and she's got nobody to sit with. Alone.
WENDY	Will I, cocker?
STEVEN	(*Angry*) Yes, you will.
WENDY	(*Angry*) Well, it won't be a first time, will it? I got used to sitting on my own at night

131

years ago, didn't I? In mourning, while you were out... swimming.

MARCUS (*Annoyed*) Will you please both be quiet. Have you no respect? This is mine and Colin's home.

STEVEN (*Angry*) What do you want me to say, Wendy? We've been through this so many times. Nobody will talk to her in the shops. Everybody avoids her like the plague. She's bored the tits off everybody, Marcus, telling them her life story. Nobody is interested in your dead... marriage, your ex-husband's boyfriends and how you've fallen in love with a first prize Turk.

WENDY (*Angry*) And why not? It's my life.

STEVEN (*Angry*) Because nobody is bloody interested in you, Wendy. Nobody cares. Your Turkish story is one of thousands of women's stories. It's written up in the Sunday Sport every Summer. It's nothing special, love... it's...

JAMIE Sad.

MARCUS (*Annoyed*) Please...

STEVEN It's boring... It's... pathetic. It's... old news.

MARCUS (*Annoyed*) I said...

WENDY	(*To Steven. Angry*) Oh, is it?
STEVEN	(*Angry*) Yes. We've seen it all before. Your behaviour.
WENDY	(*Angry*) Really?
STEVEN	(*Angry*) Yes. Seen it all fuckin' before.
WENDY	Have you?
STEVEN	Yes.
WENDY	(*Angry*) Oh well, you've seen this before, too, haven't you, Steven? My behaviour. (*Wendy stands. She picks up a bottle of wine and slowly empties it on carpet*) Cheers.
MARCUS	(*Shocked. Stands*) That's our carpet.
WENDY	(*Upset*) Oh.
MARCUS	(*Shocked*) Colin.
COLIN	(*Half asleep*) What?
MARCUS	(*Stares at carpet*) Look.
STEVEN	(*Angry. To Wendy*) Sit yourself down.
COLIN	What's up?
MARCUS	The carpet.
COLIN	(*Opens eyes*) The carpet?
MARCUS	(*Slight panic*) Yes.

133

STEVEN	Sit down I said. (*Furious*) Sit down. Sit.
WENDY	No, I won't.
STEVEN	(*Furious*) Do it.
WENDY	No.
STEVEN	(*Furious*) Yes you will.
WENDY	No I won't.
STEVEN	(*Furious*) Yes you bloody will.
WENDY	Make me.

(*Wendy continues to stand. Steven looks at her. She is defiant. Suddenly he stands, violently. Wendy moves. Steven moves. Steven and Wendy run around the room. Steven chases Wendy. He pulls her to a chair. He forces her down. Wendy screams. They fight. Violence*)

MARCUS	I don't think you should... Colin...?

(*Colin closes his eyes*)

(*Steven drags/forces Wendy into a chair*)

STEVEN	Ignore her. Take no notice. (*Furious*) She's past caring. She doesn't know what she's doing, do you? (*Shouts*) It's the pills.
MARCUS	(*Panic*) Are you alright, Wendy? (*Shakes Colin*) Colin.
COLIN	(*Half asleep*) I'm fine.

134

MARCUS   (*Angry*) Wake up. Stop them.

WENDY   (*Angry*) Don't worry. I'm used to it. His temper. Aren't I? (*Wendy gets up from chair*)

(*Steven grabs hold of Wendy. They fight. Rolling on the floor. The fight becoming almost violently sexually, frightening. Rolling on the floor.*)

     (*Screams at Steven*) Get your fuckin' hands off.

MARCUS   (*Shakes him*) Colin.

STEVEN   (*Furious. Rolling backwards and forwards across the floor with Wendy*) She only wants a reaction. Anything for a reaction. She makes me... do it, don't you, to see if I care.

WENDY   Oh, you care alright, don't you?

(*Steven violently grabs her. Pins her down*)

     (*Wendy shouts*) Get your hands off me.

STEVEN   Shut up.

WENDY   (*Angry*) He cares, don't you? The night he went out in the dark, back of a car, fiddling with a brickie.

STEVEN   (*Furious*) Shut up.

(*Marcus shakes Colin*)

MARCUS   (*Panic*) Colin.

135

WENDY   (*Angry*) Yes, while I was holding Tony's hand in the hospital. Our son, slipping away. The blip blip blip of his machine...

STEVEN   (*Anger*) Fuckin' shut it. You...

(*He pulls her hair violently from side to side*)

WENDY   Ahhhhhh...

MARCUS   (*Frightened*) Jamie, stop them.

WENDY   (*Upset. Shouts*) Couldn't get hold of you, could they? Our little boy, slipping away. Knocked over. And you were at it, weren't you? With someone else.

MARCUS   (*Frightened*) Jamie. Help me. Please.

JAMIE   (*Scared*) I... I... can't.

(*Steven holding onto Wendy's hair. Wendy tries to sit up.*)

WENDY   Bloody unnatural, he is.

STEVEN   Fuckin' shut it. Shut up I said.

WENDY   (*Shouts*) No.

MARCUS   (*Shakes Colin*) Colin.

WENDY   Bleedin' abnormal, you are, aren't you?

STEVEN   (*Furious*) Right.

(*Wendy and Steven fight*)

MARCUS   (*Frightened*) Colin. (*To Jamie*) Stop them
will you, please, Jamie. It's... our home.

(*Wendy and Steven fight more violently*)

JAMIE   (*Scared*) I can't... I can't get... involved.

(*Jamie is frightened. Almost frozen [he's seen it all before]*)

(*Steven drags Wendy around the room by her hair. Wendy
screams. Violence*)

STEVEN   (*Anger*) She'll come around. A short sharp
shock, that's what's needed. A bit of plain
speaking. A firm hand. Like a... punch bag.

(*Hits fist into his hand*)

(*Everybody watches. Shocked. Stunned. Frozen. Frightened.
But doing nothing. Colin sleeping*)

(*Shouts*) Gertcha...

(*He pushes her down. She screams. He covers her mouth with
his hand*)

Fetch some salt, Jamie.

MARCUS   Christ.

JAMIE   Salt?

STEVEN   For the carpet.

MARCUS   (*Pleads*) Colin.

(*Colin, drunk, looks at Steven and Wendy. Tries to speak*)

137

COLIN   Stop... it, will you... just... calm... down. Shhhhhh.

STEVEN   Salt, Jamie.

MARCUS   (*Closes eyes*) Oh Christ. (*Shocked. Crosses himself*) No, leave it. I'll do it. (*Opens eyes*) Just leave it. And...

WENDY   (*Shouts at Steven*) He was fuckin'... Weren't you? Fiddling about in the dark, while our son was... (Almost in tears.)

(*Jamie wanting to get out of room, quickly leaves. Wendy throws a vol au vent at Steven*)

                 (*Wendy shouts*) Bastard.

STEVEN   (*Shouts*) We've seen it all before, Wendy.

WENDY   (*Shouts*) Fuckin' shirt lifter. Arsehole rooter. (*Upset*) Oh.

(*She throws another vol au vent. Wendy in tears.*)

STEVEN   (*Sweating. He's lost it*) Nobody's interested, Wendy. Nobody's interested in your insults, are we, boys? A silly child. A little baby girl. Sticks and stones may break our bones, but names shall never... hurt us. (*Shouts violently*) Bloody woman. Stupid bitch. Fuckin' women. CUNT.

(*Steven goes to hit Wendy with his fist, a punch, violent, terrifying. But suddenly, Steven stops himself. Wendy is silently weeping. She stares at him*)

(*SILENCE*)

MARCUS   I think you should... I think we should all... Colin?

(*Colin sleeps, slumped on sofa*)

STEVEN   See, look what you've done. Are you satisfied? You've upset them, Colin and Marcus, in their new home. You've...

WENDY   (*Upset*) I've got to lie down.

(*Jamie enters*)

JAMIE   (*Nervously*) I'll rub salt into it, shall I?

COLIN   (*Half asleep*) What?

JAMIE   The carpet. She's spilt wine onto it, mate.

MARCUS   (*Angry. Shouts*) Oh sod the fuckin' carpet.

WENDY   I'm feeling...

(*Jamie rubs carpet with cloth, obediently*)

    I've got to lie down.

(*Wendy lies down on the carpet. A foetal position*)

MARCUS   Are you alright, Wendy?

WENDY   Just ignore me... Marcus.

(*Colin's head nods, slightly slumped*)

JAMIE   Is Colin alright? He's on summat, isn't he?

WENDY   It's just a phase; a phase we all go through from time to time, isn't it, Colin?... a lonely phase. (*Wendy is softly sobbing, lying on the carpet*) God just put us here for his own entertainment, didn't he, Colin, don't you think? It's his joke. (*Softly*) God's brutal.

COLIN   (*Eyes closed. Softly*) Yes.

MARCUS   (*Almost pleads*) I want you to... leave. I'd be grateful if... you'd...

STEVEN   (*Annoyed*) Are you satisfied? See? Can you hear what trouble you've caused them, Wendy? You've upset everybody.

MARCUS   (*Pleads*) It's late...

WENDY   (*Tears*) I'd like a cup of coffee... please.

MARCUS   I want you to go. I'd like you all to leave... (*Annoyed*) Please.

(*BLACKOUT*)

SCENE TWO

(*Colin lies on sofa, asleep, foetal position. Wendy lies on the floor, sleeping, foetal position. Jamie stands looking at Wendy. Steven sits watching*)

STEVEN   (*Worn out. Softly*) All I ever wanted out of life was a boy. A young boy to hold my hand. It's not much to ask for, is it? Where's the harm in it?

(*Sighs*)

Innocence.

JAMIE   We'll never budge her. She's out like a light. a dead weight. Not a pretty sight.

STEVEN   She'll come round, eventually.

JAMIE   Look at Colin. (*PAUSE*) They're nothing like last year, are they Steven, when we first met them, on the cruise? Marcus is so boring and Colin is... I didn't realise he was such a...

(*Colin sleeps [out of it]*)

STEVEN   Smackhead.

JAMIE   Do you think?

STEVEN   That didn't stop you, did it?

(*Jamie looks at Steven*)

You know what I'm talking about, sunshine.

JAMIE   Do I?

STEVEN   (*Annoyed*) Yes. I saw everything from the bathroom window. In the garden, you and him, while having a cigarette. He got stuck in, didn't he?

JAMIE   (*Feigned innocence*) Did he?

STEVEN   Yes he did. Munch munch munch. Pants around your ankles, near the bloody cows. Shaved dick and boy's bottom shining at the moon.

(*Jamie looks at Steven [boyishly]*)

JAMIE   You're still my favourite, Stevie. (*PAUSE*) Am I still your favourite? (*PAUSE*) That's what you like about me, isn't it?

STEVEN   What?

JAMIE   Me going too far.

STEVEN   Not at my expense.

JAMIE   I thought you liked watching?

STEVEN   Not when I have to stand on a toilet seat to see anything. I like it planned. I like to be there, at least.

JAMIE	When we get to New York, Steven, I can't wait to see everything with you. The Broadway shows. All those dancing boys, smiling, like you promised. White teeth and...
STEVEN	I can see right through you, Sonny Jim.
JAMIE	No you can't.
STEVEN	Oh yes I can. When you get to my age, you can see everything. (*PAUSE*) Still, that's the price I have to pay, isn't it, for liking youth. Brand new shiny things. (*Steven goes to Jamie. Steven puts his hands on Jamie's face. He turns Jamie's face around to look at him. Holds his head with his two hands, firmly*) I want to know everything, understand. I'll want to know everything about it, later on. What it felt like. Every detail, when we get to the hotel. I shall want you to tell me everything about it. You and him. What it felt like... inside.
JAMIE	I only came once.
STEVEN	I want to know. Everything.
JAMIE	One day, you'll die of a heart attack, won't you, listening to my stories?
STEVEN	Then I shall die a happy man, won't I? (*Steven lets go of Jamie. Jamie closes eyes*) Look at me.

143

(*Jamie slowly shakes head*)

> I said look at me.

(*Jamie slowly shakes head*)

> Look at me, you little...

(*Jamie looks into Steven's eyes*) (*PAUSE*)

JAMIE   Well? (*PAUSE*) Satisfied? (*Jamie looks away*)

STEVEN   Is that all I get?

JAMIE   What else do you want?

(*Jamie looks again at Steven. Jamie tentatively kisses Steven tenderly on the lips*)

> There.

STEVEN   Thank you. (*Softly*) When it's time for you to go, you will tell me, won't you?

JAMIE   I'm not going anywhere, Stevie.

STEVEN   Not yet. (*PAUSE*) I love you.

JAMIE   Thank you.

STEVEN   Is that all you've got to say?

(*PAUSE*)

JAMIE (*Softly*) I love you, too.

(*Steven begins to laugh*)

(*Uneasy*) What you laughing at?

STEVEN   What do you think? (*Steven sits*)

(*SILENCE*)

JAMIE   Where's that coffee? (*PAUSE*) I'm tired. (*Jamie yawns like a sleepy child. Then looks at Wendy*) (*PAUSE*) Whatever happens, Steven, you'll always have Wendy, won't you, to look after you? Wendy will always be there. You and her together, right up until the end.

(*Steven looks at Wendy sleeping, curled up, foetal position, on the floor*)

(*Softly*) He's always had a temper, haven't you?

(*Jamie sits next to Steven. Slowly lifts up tee shirt. Shows a bruised torso to Steven*)

Nobody knows what my boyfriend is like; what Jamie has to put up with (*Flirts*) to survive.

STEVEN   (*With affection*) Little tart.

JAMIE   I'm not ashamed. Steven likes paying for it, don't you? Makes him feel...

(*Steven tenderly kisses a bruise on Jamie's chest*)

(*Almost pained. Softly*) Tough.

145

(*Jamie lowers his tee shirt*)

(*SILENCE*)

STEVEN   Do you never think of what you're doing, what might happen to you in the future?

JAMIE   I'm never going to grow old, Steven.

STEVEN   Aren't you?

JAMIE   (*Softly*) No... I shall die... young.

(*Marcus enters with coffee pot on tray*)

MARCUS   Coffee. (*He puts tray down, begins to pour coffee*) Here you are, Wendy. Let's hope this will wake you up.

JAMIE   Is Colin alright, Marcus?

(*Marcus looks at Colin, sleeping*)

MARCUS   Yes.

JAMIE   What's he on? He's on summat, isn't he? He's been on summat all night, hasn't he?

MARCUS   Has he?

STEVEN   'Course he has.

JAMIE   You seem very calm about it, Marcus.

MARCUS   I have no option, do I? I'm used to it.

JAMIE   Used to what?

146

MARCUS	Coffee, Wendy. Wake up. Sugar? How many?
WENDY	(*Waking up*) What?
STEVEN	Coffee. How many sugars do you want?
WENDY	(*Softly*) I like it sweet.

(*Marcus puts sugar into her mug. He goes to Wendy*)

MARCUS	Here we are. Sit up. How are you feeling?
WENDY	Me, I'm fine. Why shouldn't I be?

(*Hands her coffee*)

	Ta. (*She drinks*) Much appreciated. He's a kind man, isn't he? (*She smiles*)
MARCUS	(*Looks at Colin*) I try
STEVEN	Are you going to apologise, Wendy?
WENDY	What for?
STEVEN	Lying on the floor. Your behaviour after a drink. The stain on the carpet. Manners.
WENDY	What stain?
MARCUS	It doesn't matter. Really. We'll sort it out. Me and Colin.
STEVEN	You can't carry on like this when we're away. Not on the Queen Mary.

147

WENDY   (*She drinks*) I'm sorry for the carpet. My behaviour…

MARCUS   It doesn't matter.

(*Wendy drinks*)

Wake up, Colin. Our guests are going.

(*Colin tries to sit up*)

WENDY   Have you had a good night of it, Colin?

COLIN   What? (*Waking up*) I'm fine. I feel fine. Carry on.

MARCUS   Carry on with what?

COLIN   (*Groggy*) The conversation.

MARCUS   What conversation?

COLIN   The one we're having.

JAMIE   You haven't a clue what we're saying, have you, mate? What you on?

WENDY   He's drunk too much, haven't you, love?

MARCUS   (*Almost a mutter to himself*) Amongst other things.

(*Colin slowly begins to nod on the couch. Opens eyes. Looks around him, slowly*)

WENDY   What's up? Colin? What's the matter, darling?

(Colin slowly takes hold of Wendy's hand. She doesn't understand. She looks at him. A tear falls down Colin's face)

COLIN   I'm sorry.

WENDY   Oh, what's the matter, darling?

MARCUS   *(Slightly bitter)* It makes him feel better, doesn't it, Colin, taking things until he has to wake up.

(Colin begins to slowly close his eyes)

WENDY   *(Slightly worried)* What you doing, lovie? Are you alright?

(Colin nods. Closes eyes)

JAMIE   Where you going, Col?

COLIN   *(Softly)* It's so quiet and peaceful, watching from above. *(PAUSE)* It's the colours. *(PAUSE)* The reds, blues and greens. *(PAUSE)* A kind of peace. A calmness. I can see through. Through the glass. *(He opens eyes. Colin slowly rubs forehead)* That's what we have in common, isn't it? *(He slowly rubs forehead)* We wait. *(He slowly rubs forehead)* We know it's there, in the middle of the forehead. We've seen it before and we wait to see it again. *(He slowly rubs forehead)* That point of light. *(He rubs forehead)* We wait. *(Rubs forehead)* Like in

149

the beginning, (*Rubs forehead*) when God made the world.

(*PAUSE*)

We wait... We look through the glass. And we... wait. We wait to feel it. Don't we? Again and again. We wait to feel it, again and again. The light.

(*Colin looks at Marcus*)

(*Softly*) Love.

(*Music. A long, sharp, searing note. Glass-like/angel-like. Piercing*)

(*LIGHTS FADE*)

SCENE THREE

(*LIGHTS UP*)

(*Colin sits. Marcus stands. Steven, Jamie and Wendy stand still in the shadows. They're not there. Just a presence. Like dark statues. They stare outwards (trapped in their own existence)*)

(*The sound of wind chimes*)

(*SILENCE*)

MARCUS   Where are we going?

(*PAUSE*)

COLIN   (*Softly*) I don't know.

MARCUS   What are we doing?

(*PAUSE*)

COLIN   I'm not sure.

(*SILENCE*)

You notice the quiet, don't you, when we're together? That's all that matters, isn't it?

(*PAUSE*)

I like it here. Do you? With no-one else? The silence.

(*PAUSE*)

MARCUS   Look at me.

151

(*PAUSE*)

I said look at me.

(*Marcus takes two candles. He puts candles in window. He lights them. Two candles burn in window*)

(*SILENCE*)

COLIN   I'm sorry. I've stopped. This is the last time. I've stopped. Honest. Promise. I promise.

(*Colin closes his eyes*)

MARCUS   Do you remember, Colin, the night when we first met? (*PAUSE*) I looked down from my chair, remember?

(*Colin nods*)

You were sat on the floor. You looked up at me and smiled like a child. (*PAUSE*) On your face, red, green and blue. (*PAUSE*) Disco lights. (*PAUSE*) You held my hand. (*PAUSE*) That night you whispered in my ear. You told me everything I wanted to hear. (*PAUSE*) And I felt... I felt...

COLIN   Safe. (*PAUSE*) (*Softly*) Do you think Jesus is in this house?

(*PAUSE*)

MARCUS   Yes.

(*Colin opens eyes*)

COLIN   How do you know?

MARCUS   I know.

COLIN   How can you tell?

MARCUS   Faith. (*PAUSE*) I have faith.

(*Colin stands. Walks to Marcus. Colin looks at Marcus. Marcus and Colin continue to look at each other, their eyes fixed*)

COLIN   (*Softly*) Faith.

(*Steven, Jamie, Wendy continue to stare out front*)

(*MUSIC. Brett Anderson song "Hymn"*)

(*THE LIGHT FADES SLOWLY AROUND THEM*)

(*A glass window. Two candles burn*)

(*BLACKOUT*)

THE END